SIGNIFICANT DECISIONS OF THE SUPREME COURT, 1978–1979 TERM

Bruce E. Fein

American Enterprise Institute for Public Policy Research
Washington, D.C.

Bruce E. Fein, a graduate of the University of California, Berkeley, and the Harvard Law School, is an attorney with the U.S. Department of Justice. He is a member of the Supreme Court Bar, the bars of several U.S. Courts of Appeals, the California Bar, and the American Bar Association.

The views of the author do not necessarily represent those of the U.S. Department of Justice.

ISSN 0162-0444
ISBN 0-8447-3387-3

AEI Studies 282

Printed in the United States of America

CONTENTS

1

Overview

The Jurisprudence of the Burger Court

Warren E. Burger, appointed chief justice after the close of the 1968–1969 term of the Supreme Court, concluded his first decade at the helm in 1979. An analysis of the Court's pronouncements issued during Burger's stewardship reveals three notable features. First, the Burger Court has moderated, but not disavowed, the leadership role in policy making that was characteristic of its predecessor, the Warren Court.[1] Second, the Burger Court has generally eschewed decisions that expound broad legal principles and that limit the policy discretion of subordinate federal and state courts when they confront constitutional or statutory questions; consequently, considerable judicial power has by default devolved upon the lower courts. Third, dominant recurring themes in the Burger Court's jurisprudence generally parallel sentiments of elected officials and the public, subject to important exceptions apparent in the following description of the Court's role as policy maker.

The Burger Court as Policy Maker

The Burger Court played a prominent policy-making role in several controversial areas despite vocal opposition by a substantial segment of the public. It endorsed sweeping remedial measures[2] to desegregate public schools, including the mandating of extensive busing schemes,[3]

---

[1] Justice Potter Stewart has observed that during the 1950s and 1960s, under the tutelage of Chief Justice Earl C. Warren, the Supreme Court for the first time in history assumed a leadership role in the evolution of public policy in many areas. *Newsweek*, July 4, 1976, p. 36.

[2] See Milliken v. Bradley, 433 U.S. 267 (1977).

[3] See Swann v. Charlotte-Mecklenburg Board of Education, 402 U.S. 1 (1971); Evans v. Buchanan, 393 F. Supp. 428 (D. Del.), aff'd, 423 U.S. 963 (1975); Columbus Board of Education v. Penick, 443 U.S. 449 (1979); Dayton Board of Education v. Brinkman, 443 U.S. 526 (1979).

and lightened evidentiary burdens required to justify their imposition throughout an entire school system.[4] In 1973, the Burger Court proclaimed the constitutional right to abortion.[5] In a sequel of related cases, the Court steadfastly blocked recurring state efforts to circumscribe access to an abortion by regulating the advertising of its availability,[6] the employment of abortion techniques,[7] access to contraceptives,[8] and the participation of spouses and parents of young prospective mothers in the abortion decision.[9] Going contrary to a strong tide in public opinion, the Burger Court sharply curtailed the use of capital punishment.[10] In the widely noted *Weber*[11] and *Bakke*[12] decisions, the Court blessed reverse discrimination in order to rectify historic disadvantages of minority groups. And in expounding the establishment clause of the First Amendment, the Burger Court repeatedly frustrated attempts by states to aid religiously affiliated elementary and secondary schools.[13]

These policy excursions of the Burger Court share the Warren Court's[14] activist vision of the judicial role in the governing process. Neither precedent, constitutional language, nor constitutional history offered a convincing foundation for these decisions. And with the possible exception of the abortion cases, these Burger Court rulings generally defied the majority opinion of the public at the time of the decision and frequently contravened the policy preferences of political branches of government.

---

[4] See Keyes v. School Dist. No. 1, Denver, Colorado, 413 U.S. 189 (1973); Columbus Board of Education v. Penick, 443 U.S. 449 (1979); Dayton Board of Education v. Brinkman, 443 U.S. 526 (1979).

[5] Roe v. Wade, 410 U.S. 113 (1973); Doe v. Bolton, 410 U.S. 179 (1973).

[6] See Bigelow v. Virginia, 421 U.S. 809 (1975); Carey v. Population Services International, 431 U.S. 678 (1977).

[7] See Planned Parenthood of Central Missouri v. Danforth, 428 U.S. 52 (1976).

[8] See Carey v. Population Services International, 431 U.S. 678 (1977).

[9] See Planned Parenthood of Central Missouri v. Danforth, 428 U.S. 52 (1976); Bellotti v. Baird, 443 U.S. 622.

[10] See Furman v. Georgia, 408 U.S. 238 (1972); Woodson v. North Carolina, 428 U.S. 280 (1976); Colker v. Georgia, 433 U.S. 584 (1977); Gardner v. Florida, 430 U.S. 349 (1977); Lockett v. Ohio, 438 U.S. 586 (1978).

[11] 443 U.S. 193 (1979).

[12] University of California Regents v. Bakke, 438 U.S. 265 (1978).

[13] See Lemon v. Kurtzman, 403 U.S. 602 (1971); Levitt v. Committee for Public Education and Religious Liberty, 413 U.S. 472 (1973); Committee for Public Education and Religious Liberty in Nyquist, 413 U.S. 756 (1973); Sloan v. Lemon, 413 U.S. 825 (1973); Meek v. Pittenger, 421 U.S. 349 (1975); Wolman v. Walter, 433 U.S. 229 (1977); New York v. Cathedral Academy, 434 U.S. 125 (1977).

[14] See, e.g., Baker v. Carr, 369 U.S. 189 (1962); Flast v. Cohen, 392 U.S. 83 (1968); Mapp v. Ohio, 367 U.S. 643 (1961); Gideon v. Wainwright, 372 U.S. 335 (1963); Miranda v. Arizona, 384 U.S. 436 (1966); Griswold v. Connecticut, 381 U.S. 479 (1965); Powell v. McCormack, 395 U.S. 486 (1969).

Failure to Champion Broad Constitutional or Statutory Principles

Nevertheless, the Burger Court, in comparison with the Warren Court, generally refrained from pioneering social, economic, and political decisions clothed in constitutional garb. In contrast to Warren Court decisions, moreover, its exposition of controversial constitutional and statutory interpretations was often ambiguous and was frequently limited to the particularized facts of an individual case. Its decisions regarding reverse discrimination in both *Weber* and *Bakke* and its endorsement of school busing for desegregation in *Swann* v. *Charlotte-Mecklenberg Board of Education*[15] are illustrative.[16]

In *Weber*, the Court upheld the legality of a collective-bargaining agreement that gave preferences to black employees over whites in selecting applicants for a program to teach skills required of craftworkers. The Court, however, declined to expound the demarcation between permissible and impermissible affirmative action programs. It simply noted that the contested program was unassailable because no white employees were discharged, whites were entitled to 50 percent of the training slots, the preference for blacks was temporary, and the preference was enlisted to eliminate conspicuous racial imbalance in a traditionally segregated occupation. Similarly, in *Bakke* five justices embraced the view that the equal protection clause of the Fourteenth Amendment permits some preference for blacks on account of race in evaluating applicants for higher education, but one of the five, Justice Powell, declined to state whether racial preferences would be constitutionally tolerable elsewhere. In *Swann*, the Court approved an extensive program of school busing to rectify unconstitutional segregation, but offered imprecise standards[17] for determining the propriety of other busing plans. It declared:

> No rigid guidelines as to student transportation can be given for application to the infinite variety of problems presented in thousands of situations. . . . An objection to transportation of students may have validity when the time or distance of

---

[15] 402 U.S. 1 (1971).

[16] See also Furman v. Georgia, 408 U.S. 238 (1972), and Gregg v. Georgia, 428 U.S. 153 (1976) (constitutional restraints on imposition of the death penalty); Lemon v. Kurtzman, 403 U.S. 602 (1971) (First Amendment limits on state aid to religiously affiliated schools); Hampton v. Wong, 426 U.S. 88 (1976) (due process restraints on government action).

[17] See Estes v. Metropolitan Branches of Dallas NAACP, 48 USLW 4118, 4120 (Jan. 21, 1980) (Powell, J., dissenting from dismissals of writs of certiorari as improvidently granted and observing the Court's reluctance to provide specified guidance in the formulation of desegregation decrees and noting the resulting confusion in the lower courts).

travel is so great as to either risk the health of the children or significantly impinge on the educational process. District courts must weigh the soundness of any transportation plan in light of [other factors relevant to a desegregation decree].

The narrow holdings typical of the Burger Court are partially ascribable to yawning philosophical divisions among the justices. The dissension was evident this term both in a proliferation of plurality, concurring, and dissenting opinions and in the Court's inability to forge commanding majorities behind constitutional principles.[18] The Court's disinclination to espouse clear and unequivocal constitutional doctrine had the effect of abdicating to subordinate tribunals vast discretion over the evolution of constitutional policy. The Supreme Court each year chooses to review only a small fraction of the tens of thousands of judicial decisions resting on the Constitution or federal statutes. Also, lengthy delays and costs that attend litigation discourage most parties from even bringing a case to the Supreme Court. The Burger Court's particularized jurisprudence, taken together with the practical limits on the Supreme Court's power to oversee the work of lower courts, inevitably means that enormous legal discretion lies with the subordinate federal judges and underscores the significance of the recently enacted Omnibus Judgeship Bill.[19] The act empowers President Carter, with the advice and consent of the Senate, to make appointments to 152 new federal judgeships.[20]

Dominant Themes in the Burger Court's Decisions

Putting aside some of the more celebrated cases decided during the first ten years of the Burger Court, four dominant recurring themes can be discerned. These themes, of course, do not explain or enlighten understanding of every decision. Indeed, significant rulings run contrary to these themes.[21] They do, however, embody policy choices

---

[18] See Arkansas v. Sanders, 442 U.S. 753 (1979); Caban v. Mohammed, 441 U.S. 380 (1979); County Court of Ulster County, New York v. Allen, 442 U.S. 140 (1979); Davis v. Passman, 442 U.S. 228 (1979); Gannett Co., Inc. v. DePasquale, 443 U.S. 368 (1979); Parham v. Hughes, 441 U.S. 347 (1979); Parker v. Randolph, 442 U.S. 62 (1979); Rakas v. Illinois, 439 U.S. 128 (1979); Scott v. Illinois, 440 U.S. 367 (1979); Bellotti v. Baird, 443 U.S. 622 (1979); Rose v. Mitchell, 443 U.S. 545 (1979); Dayton Board of Education v. Brinkman, 443 U.S. 526 (1979); Bell v. Wolfish, 441 U.S. 520 (1979); Jones v. Wolf, 443 U.S. 595 (1979); Mackey v. Montrym, 443 U.S. 1 (1979).
[19] Public Law 95-486, 95th Cong., 2nd sess. (1978).
[20] The legislation created 117 additional district court judgeships and 35 additional circuit court judgeships. Prior to the act, there were 400 district court judgeships and 97 circuit court judgeships.
[21] The Court's curtailment of state power under the contracts clause, Art. I, § 10, and

that are insistent influences in the Court's constitutional pronouncements. The four themes are: (1) reinvigoration of state sovereignty,
(2) narrowing access to federal judicial forums, (3) suspicion of constitutional or statutory immunities, and (4) subordination of concerns
over privacy to law enforcement needs. The remainder of this overview is devoted to a description of these themes because they have
evolved through a number of decisions, because they may well constitute the most enduring legacy of the Burger Court, and because
they have received less comment elsewhere than have the more
publicly controversial Burger Court decisions.

Reinvigorating State Sovereignty. The Burger Court has augmented
the authority of states and curtailed intrusion by both federal courts
and the Congress on state prerogatives. This has been accomplished
primarily by invoking the doctrine of abstention, by narrowing federal
habeas corpus jurisdiction, and by shielding states from congressional
dominance under the commerce clause.

In *Younger* v. *Harris*,[22] the Court concluded that principles of
equity jurisprudence and a proper respect for state functions generally
require federal courts to abstain from enjoining pending state criminal
proceedings on constitutional grounds if the plaintiff who petitions
a federal court has an opportunity to present his constitutional claims
as a defense against the prosecution. Only if a federal injunction is
necessary to forestall "great and immediate" irreparable injury, the
Court explained, can interference with the state's quest to vindicate

---

the privileges and immunities clause, Art. IV, § 2, run counter to the current of its
decisions reinvigorating state sovereignty. See United States Trust Company of New
York v. New Jersey, 431 U.S. 1 (1977) (holding that the repeal of a statutory convenant
protecting the security of bonds issued by the Port Authority of New York and New
Jersey violated the contracts clause); Allied Structural Steel Co. v. Spannaus, 438 U.S.
234 (1978) (invalidating under the contracts clause a state law that retroactively enlarged
the pension obligations of a private employer); Hicklin v. Orbeck, 437 U.S. 518 (1978)
(holding that Alaska's statutory preference for residents over nonresidents in filling
jobs stemming from the exploitation of the state's oil and gas interests contravenes the
privileges and immunities clause); Doe v. Bolton, 410 U.S. 179 (1973) (striking down
under the privileges and immunities clause a Georgia statute that permitted only
Georgia residents to obtain abortions); but see Baldwin v. Fish and Game Commission
of Montana, 436 U.S. 371 (1978) (finding no privileges and immunities clause infirmity
in Montana's discrimination against nonresidents in purchasing elk-hunting licenses).
Further, the Court in United States v. SCRAP, 412 U.S. 669 (1973), endorsed an
expansive concept of standing in upholding the right of an environmental group to
seek redress for recreational and aesthetic injuries allegedly caused by railroad rates
that encouraged the exploitation of virgin resources and discouraged the use of "re-
cyclable" materials. This decision is inconsistent with the theme of narrowing access
to the federal judiciary.
[22] 401 U.S. 37 (1971).

its criminal laws be justified. Without foreclosing the possibility of expansion, the Court identified three circumstances that would justify federal intervention under this standard: a prosecution initiated in bad faith, initiated for purposes of harassment, or initiated pursuant to a flagrantly unconstitutional statute.

The "vital consideration" underlying the abstention doctrine, the Court declared in *Younger*, is a "proper respect for state functions, a recognition of the fact that the entire country is made up of a Union of separate state governments, and a continuance of the belief that the National Government will fare best if the States and their institutions are left free to perform their separate functions in their separate ways." Echoing these sentiments, decisions following *Younger* extended its abstention principles to protect states against federal interference with judicial proceedings seeking to vindicate important state interests, irrespective of whether the proceedings are characterized as criminal, quasi-criminal, or civil. Thus, the Court held that state suits attacking a civil nuisance,[23] demanding recovery of welfare money allegedly wrongfully obtained,[24] requesting curtailment of parental rights over allegedly abused children,[25] and seeking civil contempt sanctions[26] are all shielded by the doctrine of federal abstention. The Court also expanded application of *Younger* precepts to declaratory judgment actions,[27] to federal suits filed before the commencement of a state criminal prosecution,[28] and to the formulation of equitable remedies.[29] Moreover, the extraordinary circumstances warranting federal intervention in state proceedings were narrowly confined.[30]

One consequence of *Younger* and its progeny has been an enlargement of the role of state courts in expounding federal constitutional rights. A corollary effect has been the diminution of federal supervision over the effectuation of important state policies.

In addition to invoking abstention principles, the Burger Court eclipsed federal judicial surveillance of state criminal proceedings by narrowing the scope of federal habeas corpus review. By statute,[31] federal courts are empowered to grant habeas corpus relief to state

---

[23] Huffman v. Pursue, Ltd., 420 U.S. 592 (1975).
[24] Trainor v. Hernandez, 431 U.S. 434 (1977).
[25] Judice v. Vail, 430 U.S. 327 (1977).
[26] Moore v. Sims, 442 U.S. 415 (1979).
[27] Samuels v. Mackell, 401 U.S. 66 (1971).
[28] Hicks v. Miranda, 422 U.S. 332 (1975).
[29] Rizzo v. Goode, 423 U.S. 362 (1976); O'Shea v. Littleton, 414 U.S. 488, 499–502 (1974).
[30] See, for example, Moore v. Sims, 442 U.S. 415 (1978); Trainor v. Hernandez, 431 U.S. 434 (1977); Kugler v. Helfant, 421 U.S. 117 (1975).
[31] 28 U.S. Code 2241 et seq.

prisoners whose convictions were obtained in violation of the United States Constitution. The 1963 decision in *Fay* v. *Noia*[32] sharply curtailed the circumstances under which a federal habeas court may decline to entertain on the merits constitutional claims raised by persons held in state custody. Only when a federal habeas petitioner has "deliberately by-passed" orderly procedures for presenting his constitutional claims to the state judiciary, the Court declared in *Fay*, does a federal habeas corpus judge retain discretion to refuse to consider the claims. And deliberate by-pass, the Court stated, can ordinarily be established only by showing that the federal petitioner, after consultation with counsel or otherwise, understandingly and knowingly refused the opportunity to vindicate his claims in state courts, whether for strategic, tactical, or other reasons. Adopting a crabbed interpretation of *Fay*, the Burger Court in *Stone* v. *Powell*[33] circumscribed federal habeas corpus review of exclusionary rule claims bottomed on the Fourth Amendment. Where the state has provided an opportunity for full and fair litigation of such claims, the Court held, a state prisoner may not be granted federal habeas corpus relief on the ground that evidence obtained in an unconstitutional search or seizure was introduced at his trial. In addition, the Court in *Stone* inveighed against the contention that state tribunals lack either the competence or integrity necessary to safeguard constitutional rights.[34]

The Burger Court also disavowed the exacting standards proclaimed in *Fay* for demonstrating a waiver of constitutional rights through procedural default in state courts. In *Francis* v. *Henderson*,[35] the Court held that a defendant who flouted state procedure by failing to make a pretrial challenge to the composition of a grand jury was foreclosed from belatedly asserting his constitutional claim in federal habeas proceedings, unless there was a showing of cause for the procedural default and actual prejudice. The identical cause-and-prejudice standard was applied by the Burger Court in *Wainwright* v. *Sykes*[36] to bar federal habeas review of an involuntary confession claim that state courts had refused to entertain because the defendant had failed to enter an objection during the trial. Moreover, the Court in *Wainwright* repudiated the knowing and deliberate waiver standard enunciated in *Fay*.[37] The decisions in *Stone*, *Francis*, and *Wainwright* exhibit a respect for state tribunals and procedures that was frequently

---

[32] 372 U.S. 391 (1963).
[33] 428 U.S. 465 (1976).
[34] Id. at 493 n. 35.
[35] 425 U.S. 536 (1979).
[36] 433 U.S. 72 (1977).
[37] Id. at 87–88.

lacking in the 1960s, when the Supreme Court was led by Chief Justice Earl Warren.[38]

The Burger Court also bolstered state sovereignty in its expounding of the Tenth Amendment, which declares that "powers not delegated to the United States by the Constitution, nor prohibited by it to the States, are reserved to the States respectively, or to the people." In *National League of Cities* v. *Usery*,[39] the Burger Court concluded that the amendment proscribes congressional interference under the commerce clause with state prerogatives over significant state or local government functions. This constitutional precept, the Court held, prohibited Congress from setting minimum wage and maximum hour rules for state and municipal employees under the auspices of the commerce clause. A contrary ruling, the Court maintained, would impair the states' ability to function effectively in a federal system.

In reviving the moribund Tenth Amendment to protect state prerogatives, the Court in *National League of Cities* overruled a 1968 decision[40] that sanctioned congressional regulation of the wages and hours of public school and hospital employees. *National League of Cities* also disavowed dicta in a 1936 opinion[41] asserting that Congress has plenary authority under the commerce clause to regulate state and private activities on an equal footing.

The Burger Court further buttressed state authority in *Hughes* v. *Alexandria Scrap Corp.*[42] It sustained, against commerce clause attack, a Maryland statute that imposed less exacting burdens on in-state than on out-of-state processors of abandoned vehicles seeking to qualify for a subsidy. "Nothing in the purposes animating the Commerce Clause," the Court maintained, "forbids a state, in the absence of congressional action, from participating in the market and exercising the right to favor its own citizens over others."

The enhanced respect for state government displayed by the Burger Court paralleled political and public currents outside the courthouse. In the past decade, Congress has provided generous fiscal aid to states and localities through general and special revenue-sharing statutes. Congress has enlisted the participation and enforcement authority of states to effectuate a host of federal regulatory

---

[38] See, for example, Damico v. California, 389 U.S. 416 (1967); Henry v. Mississippi, 379 U.S. 443 (1965); Dombrowski v. Pfister, 380 U.S. 479 (1965); Baggett v. Bullitt, 377 U.S. 360 (1964); Fay v. Noia, 372 U.S. 391 (1963).
[39] 426 U.S. 833 (1976).
[40] Maryland v. Wirtz, 392 U.S. 183.
[41] United States v. California, 297 U.S. 175, 185.
[42] 426 U.S. 794 (1976).

statutes, including the Clean Air Act, the Water Pollution Control Act, the Safe Drinking Water Act, the Occupational Health and Safety Act, the Surface Mining Control and Reclamation Act, and the Resources Conservation and Recovery Act. The prominent state role endorsed by Congress in the evolution and vindication of federal statutory policies is philosophically allied with the Burger Court's deference to state tribunals in expounding constitutional guarantees. Public opinion, moreover, has been receptive to elevating the stature of state governments during the 1970s. A marked growth in state budgets and employment occurred, and Jimmy Carter became the first former governor to capture the presidency since 1932.

The Burger Court's reinvigoration of state powers and prerogatives, in sum, was in concert with broader political and public currents that acknowledged the vital importance of states in our constitutional system.

Staunching Federal Litigation. Almost a century and a half ago, Alexis de Tocqueville observed that "Americans have the strange custom of seeking to settle any political or social problem by a lawsuit instead of using the political process as do people in most other countries."[43] Reflecting disapproval of this "strange custom," an array of Burger Court decisions curbed access to the federal judiciary and discouraged litigation.

The doctrine of standing was frequently invoked by the Burger Court to close the courthouse to federal plaintiffs. As delineated in *Warth* v. *Seldin*,[44] the doctrine generally requires a federal plaintiff to allege a distinct and palpable injury to himself that is likely to be redressed by a favorable decision. The requisite injury must be concrete and immediate, not speculative, and must consist of more than a generalized grievance about government operations. The Burger Court held that plaintiffs lacked standing to challenge government investigative and data-gathering activities,[45] the refusal of a state to seek criminal sanctions against fathers who defaulted on obligations to support their illegitimate children,[46] alleged constitutional infirmities in the setting of bail, assessing of court costs and sentencing,[47] a zoning ordinance that assertedly foreclosed access to low-income housing,[48] and an Internal Revenue Service regulation that relaxed

---

[43] *Democracy in America* (New York: Alfred A. Knopf, Vintage Books, 1957), p. 290.
[44] 422 U.S. 490 (1975).
[45] Laird v. Tatum, 408 U.S. 1 (1972).
[46] Linda R. S. v. Richard D., 410 U.S. 614 (1973).
[47] O'Shea v. Littleton, 414 U.S. 488 (1974).
[48] Warth v. Seldin, 422 U.S. 490 (1975).

the obligations of hospitals to provide free or low-cost medical care in order to obtain tax-exempt status.[49] Furthermore, the Burger Court confined the standing of taxpayers to assail government action within the narrow limits set by the 1968 decision in *Flast* v. *Cohen*.[50] There the Court permitted a federal taxpayer in the capacity of taxpayer to challenge a federal spending statute on the ground that it violated the establishment clause of the First Amendment. The Burger Court, however, denied standing to federal taxpayers who questioned the constitutionality of a statute empowering the Central Intelligence Agency to account for its expenditures simply on the certificate of the director.[51] In another case, standing was denied when taxpayers challenged the constitutionality of the holding by incumbent congressmen of commissions in the armed forces reserve.[52]

Closely related to the doctrine of standing is the doctrine of political questions. Derived from the separation of powers among the three branches of the federal government, the doctrine obliges the federal judiciary to defer to the political branches on questions inappropriate for judicial review. Such political questions occur in cases in which one or more of the following are judged to exist:[53]

1. a textually demonstrable constitutional commitment of the disputed issue to a coordinate political department
2. a lack of judicially discoverable and manageable standards for resolving the dispute
3. the impossibility of deciding the issue without an initial policy determination of a kind clearly most appropriate to the discretion of the political branches
4. the impossibility of a court decision that would be properly respectful of the coordinate branches of government
5. an unusual need for unquestioning adherence to a political decision already made
6. the potential for embarrassment from multifarious pronouncements by various departments on the identical question.

The 1969 decision of the Warren Court in *Powell* v. *McCormack*[54] sharply compressed the political questions doctrine and seemingly placed only a handful of constitutional disputes outside the cognizance of the federal judiciary. The Court declared that Congressman

---

[49] Simon v. Eastern Kentucky Welfare Rights Organization, 426 U.S. 26 (1976).
[50] 392 U.S. 83.
[51] United States v. Richardson, 418 U.S. 166 (1974).
[52] Schlesinger v. Reservists Committee to Stop the War, 418 U.S. 208 (1974).
[53] Baker v. Carr, 369 U.S. 186 (1962).
[54] 395 U.S. 489.

Adam Clayton Powell had been unconstitutionally excluded from the 90th Congress since he satisfied the age, citizenship, and residency standards contained in Article I, section 2, of the Constitution. The Burger Court has revived the doctrine of political questions, holding that a suit seeking continued judicial surveillance over the National Guard to ensure compliance with standards concerning training and weapons presented a political question beyond the purview of the federal judiciary.[55] A plurality of the Court also declared that a challenge by members of Congress to the authority of the president to terminate unilaterally a defense treaty is nonjusticiable.[56]

Federal jurisdictional statutes have been narrowly construed[57] by the Burger Court, reflecting its unhappiness over the reflexive employment of the federal judiciary to litigate grievances. The Burger Court also discouraged lawsuits by limiting the inherent judicial authority to award attorney fees,[58] saddling class action plaintiffs with a variety of procedural burdens,[59] and refusing to offer any general constitutional relief against the payment of modest fees by indigents seeking access to the judiciary.[60] And a due process right of immediate access to state courts to obtain a divorce was abruptly denied.[61] In sum, a prominent undercurrent in the Burger Court's jurisprudence has been the effort to encourage use of nonjudicial forums to resolve disputes or to alter laws that have evoked dissatisfaction.[62] It implicitly questions whether the wisdom, competence, and efficiency of the judiciary exceeds that of other institutions.[63]

The Burger Court's quest to curtail litigation has paralleled the policies of recent federal and state statutes, the search by the bar for nonjudicial techniques for settling disputes, and a growing public concern about an "imperial judiciary." The 1974 Federal Trade Commission Improvements Act[64] announced a congressional policy "to

---

[55] Gilligan v. Morgan, 413 U.S. 1 (1973).
[56] Goldwater v. Carter, 48 USLW 3402, December 13, 1979 (plurality opinion of Justice Rehnquist).
[57] Zahn v. International Paper Co., 414 U.S. 291 (1973); Aldinger v. Howard, 427 U.S. 1 (1976); Johnson v. Mississippi, 421 U.S. 213 (1975); Owen Equipment and Erection Co. v. Kroger, 437 U.S. 365 (1978).
[58] Alyeska Pipeline Service Co. v. The Wilderness Society, 421 U.S. 240 (1975).
[59] Eisen v. Carlisle & Jacquelin, 417 U.S. 156 (1974); Oppenheimer Fund, Inc. v. Sanders, 437 U.S. 340 (1978); Zahn v. International Paper Co., 414 U.S. 291 (1973); Coopers & Lybrand v. Livesay, 437 U.S. 436 (1978).
[60] Compare United States v. Kras, 409 U.S. 434 (1973), and Ortwein v. Schwab, 410 U.S. 656 (1973), with Boddie v. Connecticut, 401 U.S. 371 (1971).
[61] Sosna v. Iowa, 419 U.S. 393 (1975).
[62] See Warth v. Seldin, 422 U.S. 490, 508 n. 18 (1975).
[63] See Schlesinger v. Reservists Committee to Stop the War, 418 U.S. 208, 222 (1974).
[64] P. L. 93-637, 15 U.S. Code 2310(a) (1976).

encourage warrantors to establish procedures whereby consumer disputes are fairly and expeditiously settled through informal dispute settlement mechanisms." It empowers the Federal Trade Commission to prescribe minimum standards for any informal dispute settlement procedure incorporated in certain warranties. Consumers must resort to settlement procedures satisfying such standards before pursuing specified legal remedies in judicial forums. The Dispute Resolution Act of 1980[65] authorizes federal grants to states, localities, and non-profit organizations to explore and experiment with nonjudicial mechanisms for resolving minor disputes. Several states require or authorize resort to arbitration or conciliation before malpractice actions may be filed in court. The Law Enforcement Assistance Administration has funded three neighborhood justice centers in searching for effective nonjudicial strategies to litigation. Similarly, a special committee of the American Bar Association is intensively exploring nonjudicial techniques for composing minor controversies. Finally, both scholars and the popular media have expressed apprehension in recent years that excessive judicial interference with government action could damage the democratic process and paralyze policy makers.

Suspicion of Constitutional or Statutory Immunities. A third signal feature of Burger Court decisions has been unfriendliness toward assertions of government or official immunities. This posture has been most pronounced with respect to immunities claimed by federal officials.

The Burger Court's ruling in *United States* v. *Nixon*[66] held that presidential claims of executive privilege are subject to judicial review. The Court asserted, moreover, that the privilege must yield to a specific need for evidence in a criminal trial when invoked simply to protect a generalized interest in the confidentiality of presidential communications. Thus, the Court ordered President Nixon to comply with Special Prosecutor Jaworski's demand for sixty-four presidential tape recordings and various documents for use in the so-called Watergate cover-up trial.

Executive immunity was further eroded in *Butz* v. *Economou.*[67] There the Burger Court proclaimed that federal executive officials are generally entitled to only a qualified immunity from damage suits founded on alleged violations of constitutional rights. Executive of-

---

[65] P.L. 96-190, 96th Cong., 2nd sess. (February 12, 1980).
[66] 418 U.S. 683 (1974).
[67] 438 U.S. 478 (1978).

ficers enjoy absolute immunity, however, for actions undertaken to prosecute or adjudicate administrative or other complaints. The *Butz* decision was foreshadowed by the Burger Court's earlier ruling in *Bivens* v. *Six Unknown Agents*[68] that the Fourth Amendment creates a private damage action against federal officers who flout its injunction against unreasonable searches and seizures. And a distaste for absolute immunity was manifest last term in *Davis* v. *Passman.*[69] The Court held that the Fifth Amendment creates a private damage action against a congressman for acts of unconstitutional sex discrimination in selecting legislative assistants.

Members of Congress were frequently rebuffed by the Burger Court in assertions of immunity under the speech or debate clause, Article I, section 6 of the Constitution. Generally speaking, the clause proscribes either executive or judicial questioning of acts by any member that are integral to participation in those deliberative and communicative processes of Congress that bear on its legislative or other constitutional functions. The Burger Court repeatedly rejected the view that the communications of a member of Congress with his constituents, the press, or the public are protected by the speech or debate clause.[70] In addition, the Court held that the clause is no barrier to prosecuting a congressman for taking a bribe offered to influence his legislative acts.[71]

With regard to nonconstitutional wrongful acts, the Burger Court has hewed to a restrained conception of official immunity. It explained in *Doe* v. *McMillan*[72] that absolute immunity from damages would be recognized only for actions whose contribution "to effective government in particular contexts outweighs the perhaps recurring harm to individual citizens. . . ." Applying this standard, the Court denied absolute immunity to officials of the Government Printing Office for printing and distributing an allegedly defamatory congressional committee report.

States have enjoyed greater success than national officials in retaining constitutional and statutory immunities. This reflects in part the Burger Court's deference to state powers and prerogatives.

The Eleventh Amendment, as expounded in a long line of decisions, offers states immunity from private damage suits in federal courts, unless there is a waiver. In *Edelman* v. *Jordan,*[73] the Burger

---

[68] 403 U.S. 388 (1971).
[69] 442 U.S. 228 (1979).
[70] Gravel v. United States, 408 U.S. 606 (1972); Hutchinson v. Proxmire, 443 U.S. 111 (1979).
[71] United States v. Brewster, 408 U.S. 501 (1972).
[72] 412 U.S. 306 (1973).
[73] 415 U.S. 651 (1974).

Court held that the amendment barred the award by a federal court of retroactive welfare benefits that had been wrongfully denied by the state. Although the welfare program was established under federal auspices and received federal funds, the Court rejected the argument that Congress had conditioned state participation on waiver of Eleventh Amendment immunity. Congress must mandate waiver either in express language or through unambiguous implication, the Court insisted, in order to hold a state responsible.

The generous conception of state immunity displayed in *Edelman*, however, was tempered by a series of other decisions. The immunity of the Eleventh Amendment, the Burger Court ruled, is not assertable by a local school board[74] or a bistate planning commission.[75] The Court also held that the amendment is no obstacle to awarding of attorney's fees against a state,[76] to requiring states to fund such compensatory education programs as are necessary to eradicate vestiges of unconstitutional school segregation,[77] or to obligating states to apprise welfare recipients of an administrative forum to process claims for benefits wrongfully denied.[78] Congress is empowered under section 5 of the Fourteenth Amendment, the Burger Court further ruled, to abrogate Eleventh Amendment immunity in order to fortify constitutional rights against state infringement.[79]

State officials and localities also fared poorly in seeking immunity from the federal protection of constitutional rights enshrined in 42 U.S. Code, section 1983. Generally speaking, that statute offers a damage remedy against any person who violates another's constitutional rights. The Burger Court held that virtually all state executive officers, including a governor, are answerable in damages under the statute for constitutional wrongdoing, unless good faith can be shown. But prosecutors and judges, the Court ruled, enjoy absolute damage immunity for acts taken in the furtherance of their official duties.[80]

Overruling a 1961 decision, the Burger Court denied municipalities absolute immunity for constitutional wrongdoing under section 1983.[81] It indicated, however, in *Quern v. Jordan*[82] that states are clothed with absolute immunity, and held that regional legislators

---

[74] Mt. Healthy City Board of Education v. Doyle, 429 U.S. 274 (1977).
[75] Lake Country Estates v. Tahoe Regional Planning Commission, 440 U.S. 391 (1979).
[76] Hutto v. Finney, 437 U.S. 678 (1978).
[77] Milliken v. Bradley, 433 U.S. 267 (1977).
[78] Quern v. Jordan, 440 U.S. 332 (1979).
[79] Fitzpatrick v. Bitzer, 427 U.S. 445 (1976).
[80] Imbler v. Pachtman, 424 U.S. 409 (1976); Stump v. Sparkman, 435 U.S. 349 (1978).
[81] Monell v. Department of Social Services, 436 U.S. 658 (1978).
[82] See note 78, supra.

are not accountable in damages for legislative acts that violate the Constitution.[83]

The predilections of the Burger Court toward assertions of government immunity are underscored by its emphatic quotation in *Butz v. Economou*[84] from a century-old decision:[85]

> No man in this country is so high that he is above the law. No officers of the law may set that law at defiance with impunity. All officers of the government from the highest to the lowest are creatures of the law, and are bound to obey it.

These sentiments undoubtedly spring from judicial apprehension that official authority may be abused and that legal restraints are necessary to deter and to rectify overzealous, oppressive, or corrupt deeds. A similar mistrust of government and elected representatives has increasingly become a significant part of public and political attitudes. At the national level, the crimes and transgressions unearthed by the Watergate investigations spurred the enactment of the Federal Election Campaign Act Amendments of 1974,[86] the Ethics in Government Act,[87] and the Inspector General Act.[88] The first tightly regulates the financing of federal elections and provides public funds for presidential aspirants. The Ethics in Government Act establishes a mechanism for the appointment of a special prosecutor to investigate allegations of misconduct lodged against important government or political party officials. It also requires extensive financial disclosure statements by high government officials and restricts former officials in dealings with federal agencies to forestall even an appearance of impropriety. The Inspector General Act creates an Office of Inspector General in each of twelve government agencies to audit government programs and to prevent and detect fraud and abuse. In addition, Congress recently abrogated the defense of sovereign immunity in suits against the United States seeking injunctive relief and assailing the legality of actions taken by government agencies.[89] Fears of electronic surveillance and wiretapping abuses prompted enactment of the Foreign Intelligence Surveillance Act.[90] Recognizing the abuses that sprang from J. Edgar Hoover's omnipotent control over the FBI,

---

[83] See note 54, supra.
[84] 438 U.S. 478, 506 (1978).
[85] United States v. Lee, 106 U.S. 196 (1882).
[86] P.L. 93-433.
[87] P.L. 95-521.
[88] P.L. 95-452.
[89] P.L. 94-574 (1976).
[90] P.L. 95-511 (1978).

15

Congress enacted a ten-year limit on the term of any FBI director.[91] Revelations of widespread Central Intelligence Agency misdeeds prompted the enactment of a statute and the issuance of an executive order to enhance accountability for its operations and to limit its powers.[92]

At the state and local levels of government, the decade witnessed a proliferation of laws regulating campaign contributions and expenditures. Financial disclosure obligations of various sorts were also placed on state and local officials. And the hoary doctrines of state and municipal government immunity were severely eroded by state courts and legislatures.[93]

These legislative, executive, and judicial actions that seek to check government misconduct have marched in step with public opinion. Confidence in the competence and integrity of governmental institutions and officials has plummeted in recent years. President Carter dwelled at length on this so-called crisis of confidence in his nationwide television address delivered on July 15, 1979.

Subordination of Privacy to Law Enforcement. A fourth prominent feature of Burger Court decisions has been a subordination of privacy to the perceived needs of law enforcement. The Court's exposition of the Fourth Amendment's proscription of unreasonable searches and seizures exemplifies this tendency quite clearly.

Ordinarily, the amendment requires a warrant founded on probable cause and issued by a neutral magistrate before officials can search for evidence of crime.[94] These requirements, the Burger Court declared in *United States* v. *United States District Court*,[95] are based on the belief "that unreviewed executive discretion may yield too readily to pressures to obtain incriminating evidence and overlook potential invasions of privacy and protected speech." Nevertheless, the Court sustained several official searches conducted without warrants: border searches,[96] routine inventory searches of a detained auto,[97]

---

[91] P.L. 94-503, Title II, section 203(b) (1978).

[92] 22 U.S. Code 2422; see Executive Order 12036 (Jan. 25, 1978).

[93] As of 1978, 46 states had abrogated or significantly limited their sovereign immunity by judicial decree, statutory reform, or constitutional amendment. See K. Davis, Administrative Law Treatise, Section 25.00 (1978 Supplement), and Senate Committee on the Judiciary, Judicial Review of Agency Action, Senate Report No. 996, 94th Congress, 2nd sess. (1976).

[94] See Almeida-Sanchez v. United States, 413 U.S. 266 (1973).

[95] 407 U.S. 297 (1972).

[96] United States v. Ramsey, 431 U.S. 606 (1977).

[97] South Dakota v. Opperman, 428 U.S. 364 (1976).

searches of extensively regulated businesses,[98] caseworker visits to homes of welfare recipients,[99] searches at fixed traffic checkpoints to detect immigration violations,[100] and full searches of arrestees without even suspicion that weapons or evidence of crime would be discovered.[101]

The Fourth Amendment also forbids unreasonable arrests or detention. Discounting privacy interests, the Burger Court held that persons may be arrested in public places without warrants,[102] or arrested solely on the basis of an information issued by a prosecutor,[103] without breaching the constitutional norm of reasonableness.

In 1967 the Court declared that Fourth Amendment guarantees extend to reasonable expectations of privacy.[104] A twofold inquiry is necessary to determine whether an expectation of privacy is reasonable: first, a person must exhibit a subjective expectation of privacy; and, second, society must be prepared to recognize that expectation as reasonable.[105] Applying this test, the Burger Court held that individuals lack any Fourth Amendment protection against government seizures of personal financial records maintained by banks,[106] against the installation of pen registers to record numbers dialed from private residences,[107] or against the use of concealed transmitters by informants to convey conversations to police agents.[108] And a passenger in a car, the Burger Court declared this term, ordinarily cannot invoke the Fourth Amendment to challenge a police search of the vehicle.[109] The Burger Court also concluded that persons have no interest protected by the Fourth Amendment in withholding voice[110] or handwriting[111] exemplars from grand juries. In other seminal decisions, the Court ruled that the Fourth Amendment does not preclude covert entries to install electronic surveillance devices,[112] search warrants

---

[98] United States v. Biswell, 406 U.S. 311 (1972); Colonnade Catering Corp. v. United States, 397 U.S. 72 (1970).
[99] Wyman v. James, 400 U.S. 309 (1971).
[100] United States v. Martinez-Fuerte, 428 U.S. 543 (1976).
[101] United States v. Robinson, 414 U.S. 218 (1973).
[102] United States v. Watson, 423 U.S. 411 (1976).
[103] Gerstein v. Pugh, 420 U.S. 103 (1975).
[104] Katz v. United States, 389 U.S. 347.
[105] Id. at 361 (Harlan, J. concurring).
[106] United States v. Miller, 425 U.S. 435 (1976).
[107] Smith v. Maryland, 442 U.S. 735 (1979).
[108] United States v. White, 401 U.S. 745 (1971).
[109] Rakas v. Illinois, 439 U.S. 128 (1979).
[110] United States v. Dionisio, 419 U.S. 1 (1973).
[111] United States v. Mara, 410 U.S. 19 (1973).
[112] Dalia v. United States, 441 U.S. 238 (1979).

directed against persons not suspected of crime,[113] or automatic cavity searches of prison inmates following contact visits.[114]

The Burger Court's enthronement of law enforcement needs over privacy has not been confined to the Fourth Amendment. The Court endorsed a cramped conception of the Fifth Amendment privilege against compulsory self-incrimination, denying the privilege if government investigators avoid compelling the suspect to disclose testimonial evidence.[115] It also denied constitutional redress to persons defamed by false criminal accusations disseminated by the police.[116]

In contrast to the Burger Court's marked subordination of privacy values to law enforcement needs, political and public sentiments are ambivalent. During the past decade, soaring crime rates, persistent criminal recidivism, and the spectacle of increasing numbers of violent juveniles have provoked a variety of statutory responses sympathetic to law enforcement concerns: mandatory minimum sentencing provisions, capital punishment statutes, and harsher treatment of juvenile criminals. On the other hand, a rising tide of concern over invasions of privacy emerged during the 1970s. Restrictions on the preparation, maintenance, and disclosure of government and educational records pertaining to individuals were enacted by Congress in 1974 in the Privacy Act[117] and the Family Educational Rights and Privacy Act.[118] Congress also erected certain protections against official access to bank records in the Right of Financial Privacy Act of 1978.[119] Similar bank record legislation was enacted in California.[120] Threats to privacy posed by wiretapping and electronic surveillance were partially responsible for the controls imposed by the Foreign Intelligence Surveillance Act. Public opinion polls and the recent report of the congressionally created Privacy Protection Study Commission confirm a significant national concern over protection of individual privacy.

The Burger Court's exposition of the Fourth Amendment and the Court's general subordination of concerns for privacy to law enforcement needs seems marginally misaligned with prevailing public

---

[113] Zurcher v. Standford Daily, 436 U.S. 547 (1978).
[114] Bell v. Wolfish, 441 U.S. 520 (1979).
[115] See, e.g., Fisher v. United States, 425 U.S. 391 (1976); Andresen v. Maryland, 427 U.S. 463 (1976).
[116] Paul v. Davis, 424 U.S. 693 (1976).
[117] P.L. 93-579.
[118] P.L. 93-380, Title V, section 513(a).
[119] P.L. 95-630.
[120] See California Right to Financial Privacy Act of 1976, "Government," California Annotated Code, section 7460 et seq.

opinion. The latter counsels greater deference to privacy in the constitutional balance.

Conclusion

Internal conflicts and ambiguities pervade the jurisprudence of the Burger Court. It exhibits no impassioned devotion to any constitutional ideal that compares with the quest for equality pursued by the Warren Court. The recurring themes of the Burger Court identified in this overview do not reflect constitutional values that pervasively dominate the Court's thinking. Furthermore, Burger Court decisions are not renowned for their scholarship or deference to precedent. They portray a court equivocal in its oft-professed commitment to judicial restraint and irresolute in its constitutional pronouncements.

These attributes of the Burger Court have their counterparts in Congress and the executive branch. Over the past decade, the elective branches of government have failed to offer decisive leadership and to forge a national consensus on major issues of public policy. The nation's energy policy, for instance, has been confounded by the conflicting aims of reducing dependence on foreign sources of oil and gas, depressing the price of domestic sources of energy below world prices, encouraging conservation, and ensuring adequate energy supplies. Similarly, the 1970s left economic policy makers in disarray in offering various incompatible prescriptions to control inflation without excessive unemployment: mandatory wage-price controls, voluntary wage-price guidelines, restrictive monetary policy, a balanced federal budget, constitutional and statutory ceilings on government spending, tax cuts, and tax increases.

The intellectual and philosophical contradictions in the decisions of the Burger Court support the observation of Justice Benjamin Cardozo that "the great tides and currents which engulf the rest of men, do not turn aside in their course, and pass the judges by."[121]

Voting Alignments

In cases concerning the administration of criminal justice and a broad spectrum of civil rights and civil liberties, the voting patterns of Justices Powell and Stewart changed notably from the 1977–1978 term. A selected sample of nineteen nonunanimous decisions re-

---

[121] B. Cardozo, *The Nature of the Judicial Process* (New Haven, Connecticut: Yale University Press, 1921), p. 168.

19

Table 1
ACTION OF INDIVIDUAL JUSTICES

	Opinions Written[a]				Dissenting Votes[b] in Disposition by		
	Opinions of Court	Concur-rences	Dis-sents[c]	Total	Opinion	Memoran-dum	Total
Blackmun	13	18	10	41	14	5	19
Brennan	13	7	21	41	47	4	51
Burger	17	6	1	24	21	4	25
Marshall	13	4	15	32	48	3	51
Powell	12	11	17	40	19	3	22
Rehnquist	16	12	12	40	29	14	43
Stevens	15	7	13	35	27	5	32
Stewart	15	10	20	45	35	7	42
White	16	3	13	32	19	5	24
Per curiam	8	—	—	8	—	—	—
Total	138	78	122	338	259	50	309

Note: A complete explanation of the way in which the tables are compiled may be found in "The Supreme Court, 1967 Term," *Harvard Law Review,* vol. 82 (1968), pp. 93, 301–2, and "The Supreme Court, 1969 Term," *Harvard Law Review,* vol. 84 (1970), pp. 30, 254–55.

Table 1, with the exception of the dissenting votes portion, deals only with full-opinion decisions disposing of cases on their merits. Eight per curiam decisions were long enough to be considered full opinions. The memorandum tabulations include memorandum orders disposing of cases on the merits by affirming, reversing, vacating, or remanding. They exclude orders disposing of petitions for certiorari, dismissing writs of certiorari as improvidently granted, dismissing appeals for lack of jurisdiction or for lack of a substantial federal question, and disposing of miscellaneous applications. Certified questions are not included.

[a] A concurrence or dissent is recorded as a written opinion whenever a reason, however brief, is given, except when simply noted by the reporter.

[b] A justice is considered to have dissented when he voted to dispose of the case in any manner different from that of the majority of the Court.

[c] Opinions concurring in part and dissenting in part are counted as dissents.

Source: *Harvard Law Review,* vol. 93 (November 1979), p. 275.

garding the criminal justice system showed that Powell evenly divided his votes between the government and the accused or inmate. During the preceding term, Powell favored the government in eleven of seventeen selected nonunanimous decisions. Stewart, in contrast, voted eleven to seven in favor of the government this term, whereas he rejected government arguments in nine of seventeen selected cases during the 1977–1978 term.

Both Powell and Stewart displayed increased hostility to claims of civil rights and civil liberties. In a selected sample of twenty nonunanimous decisions, Powell cast but two votes to sustain such

Table 2
DISPOSITION OF CASES: 1978, 1977, AND 1976
OCTOBER TERMS

	1978	1977	1976
Paid Cases			
Cases from prior terms	434	472	452
Cases docketed during term	1,949	1,841	1,872
Cases on docket	2,383	2,313	2,324
Cases granted review and carried over	66	78	90
Cases denied, dismissed or withdrawn	1,732	1,652	1,620
Cases summarily decided	79	71	162
Cases granted review this term	144	145	147
Cases acted upon	2,021	1,946	2,019
Cases not acted upon	362	367	305
In Forma Pauperis Cases			
Cases from prior terms	392	334	398
Cases docketed during term	1,939	1,992	2,000
Cases on docket	2,331	2,326	2,398
Cases granted review and carried over	8	10	8
Cases denied, dismissed or withdrawn	1,938	1,898	2,013
Cases summarily decided	31	13	40
Cases granted review this term	19	14	22
Cases acted upon	1,996	1,935	2,083
Cases not acted upon	335	391	315
Original Cases			
Cases from prior terms	12	8	7
Cases docketed during term	5	6	1
Cases on docket	17	14	8
Cases disposed of during term	0	3	2
Cases remaining	17	11	6
Total cases on docket	4,731	4,653	4,730
Argument Calendar			
Cases available at beginning of term	75	88	99
Cases made available during term	163	159	169
Cases reset for argument	8	9	0
Original cases set for argument	3	2	1
Total cases available for argument	249	258	269

21

Table 2 (continued)
DISPOSITION OF CASES: 1978, 1977, AND 1976
OCTOBER TERMS

	1978	1977	1976
Cases argued	168	172	176
Dismissed or remanded without argument	2	13	5
Total cases disposed of	170	185	181
Total cases available	79	73	88
Decision Calendar			
Cases argued and submitted	168	172	176
Disposed of by signed opinion	153[a]	141	154
Disposed of by per curiam opinion	8[b]	8	22
Set for reargument	8	9	0
Total cases decided	168	159	176
Cases awaiting decision	0	13	0
Number of signed opinions	130	117	126

[a] Includes No. 78 Original.
[b] Includes No. 8 Original.
Source: Office of the Clerk of the Supreme Court of the United States.

claims, whereas he divided his votes evenly in the prior term. Stewart supported civil rights proponents on only four occasions, in contrast to nine favorable votes in sixteen selected nonunanimous decisions during the preceding term. In sum, Stewart and Powell both assumed a more "conservative" posture in their approach to civil rights this term; Stewart also carried this posture into the criminal justice field, whereas Powell displayed more "liberal" inclinations there.

The voting patterns of the seven other justices remained relatively unchanged from the preceding term.[122] In the realm of criminal justice, Rehnquist, Burger, and Blackmun solidly supported the government, whereas Brennan, Marshall, and Stevens were steadfast in opposition. A selected sample of nineteen cases revealed that Rehnquist cast all his votes in favor of the government, joined by Burger on sixteen occasions and by Blackmun on fourteen. Brennan and Marshall opposed the government in every case and lost Stevens as an ally only three times. White split his votes thirteen to five in support of the government.

---

[122] See B. Fein, *Significant Decisions of the Supreme Court, 1977–1978 Term* (Washington, D.C.: American Enterprise Institute, 1979), p. 18.

In the area of civil rights jurisprudence, a selected sample of twenty cases continued to show polarization on the Court. Rehnquist voted only once with civil rights advocates, who managed only two votes from Burger. In contrast, Marshall championed civil rights in all twenty cases, and was joined by Brennan and White eighteen and thirteen times, respectively. Blackmun cast twelve votes favorable to civil rights, and Stevens, ten.

1978–1979 Statistics

The caseload of the Supreme Court increased slightly from the preceding term. The total number of cases on dockets grew from 4,653 to 4,731. The Court heard 168 cases argued, disposed of 153 by signed opinion, and summarily decided 110. The corresponding figures for the 1977–1978 term were 172 cases argued, 141 disposed of by signed opinion, and 84 summarily decided cases.

2
Summaries of Significant Decisions

Criminal Law: Powers of the Police and Prosecutors

The Fourth Amendment was the central focus in numerous Court decisions examining a variety of investigatory and prosecutorial powers. Crafted to safeguard privacy without subordinating the reasonable needs of law enforcement, the amendment has been plagued by interpretive uncertainties. Privacy concerns and law enforcement needs have won alternating victories in particular cases.[1] The Burger Court has generally held privacy subservient to law enforcement,[2] albeit with some significant exceptions.[3] The 1978–1979 term continued to sound this theme, but in a softer tone.

Champions of privacy were handed a trio of sharp defeats as the Court narrowed the scope of protection offered by the Fourth Amendment. In *Smith* v. *Maryland*, 422 U.S. 735 (1979), a 5–3 majority held that the installation and use of a pen register by police to record

---

[1] Compare, e.g., Almeida-Sanchez v. United States, 413 U.S. 266 (1973) (holding unconstitutional a warrantless search of an auto twenty-five miles north of the Mexican border as part of a scheme to detect illegal aliens) with United States v. Martinez-Fuerte, 428 U.S. 543 (1976) (sanctioning the operation of permanent traffic checkpoints inland from the Mexican border to detect illegal immigration).
[2] See, e.g., United States v. Biswell, 406 U.S. 311 (1972) (upholding warrantless searches of business premises for records and merchandise of firearms dealers); United States v. Miller, 425 U.S. 435 (1976) (holding that persons lack any reasonable expectation of privacy concerning bank records); United States v. Robinson, 414 U.S. 218 (1973) (sanctioning full police searches after custodial arrest irrespective of whether weapons or evidence of crime justifying the arrest are sought).
[3] See United States v. U.S. District Court, 407 U.S. 297 (1972) (holding unconstitutional warrantless employment of electronic surveillance to investigate domestic threats to the national security); Marshall v. Barlow's, Inc., 436 U.S. 307 (1978) (holding unconstitutional warrantless inspections of business premises by officers enforcing the Occupational Health and Safety Act); Mincey v. Arizona, 437 U.S. 385 (1978) (condemning a warrantless search of an apartment to solve a crime of murder).

24

telephone dialings is unconstrained by the amendment. Writing for the Court, Justice Blackmun maintained that telephone subscribers lack any general expectation that the numbers they dial will remain secret. In addition, Blackmun asserted, society would not accept such an expectation of privacy as reasonable.

A divided Court in *Rakas* v. *Illinois*, 439 U.S. 128 (1979), also embraced a crabbed conception of privacy expectations. A 5–4 majority, speaking through Justice Rehnquist, ruled that passengers in automobiles ordinarily lack Fourth Amendment protection against searches of the car. Disavowing a dictum in *Jones* v. *United States*, 362 U.S. 257 (1960), that persons "legitimately on the premises where a search occurs" may assail its legality under the Fourth Amendment, Rehnquist asserted that legitimate presence is but one factor in determining whether a protectable privacy interest has been invaded.

The capstone of the Court's subjugation of privacy was set in place in *Dalia* v. *United States*, 441 U.S. 238 (1979). Justice Powell, writing for a 5–4 majority, held baseless a Fourth Amendment objection to the action of police in covertly entering private premises to install electronic surveillance devices, noting that the use of "bugging" devices had been authorized by a warrant. Powell maintained that covert entry, in itself, required no explicit sanction in a warrant, because the executing officers are entrusted with discretion to choose among procedures to install approved electronic devices.

The Court, however, strongly supported privacy in six other important decisions expounding the Fourth Amendment. Speaking three times with unanimity through Chief Justice Burger, the Court condemned a brief police detention not justified by reasonable suspicion of wrongdoing, *Brown* v. *Texas*, 443 U.S. 47 (1979), inveighed against an open-ended search warrant for obscene materials and judicial participation in its execution, *Lo-Ji Sales, Inc.* v. *New York*, 442 U.S. 319 (1979), and nullified a Puerto Rican statute authorizing blanket searches of the luggage of persons arriving from the United States, *Torres* v. *Puerto Rico*, 442 U.S. 465 (1979). The Court also twice forged commanding majorities in denouncing searches and seizures without warrants. By a 7–2 margin, the Court held that a warrantless search of a suitcase discovered in an automobile ran afoul of the Fourth Amendment, *Arkansas* v. *Sanders*, 442 U.S. 753 (1979). An 8–1 majority assailed random police stops of motor vehicles to enforce traffic laws as an unreasonable invasion of privacy, *Delaware* v. *Prouse*, 440 U.S. 648 (1979).

The Court further buttressed the protections of the Fourth Amendment in *Dunaway* v. *New York*, 442 U.S. 200 (1979). Justice Brennan, writing for a 6–2 majority, declared that the Fourth Amendment proscribed custodial questioning by the police based on acts falling short of the probable cause needed for a formal arrest. In contrast, *Michigan* v. *DeFillippo*, 443 U.S. 31 (1979), witnessed the ascendency of law enforcement considerations in Fourth Amendment interpretation. By a 6–3 vote, the Court found no constitutional barrier to the introduction of evidence discovered pursuant to a good-faith arrest, even though based on an ordinance subsequently held unconstitutional.

Waiver of Fifth and Sixth Amendment Rights. Two 1978–1979 term decisions underscored the Court's resolve to circumscribe[4] the controversial ruling in *Miranda* v. *Arizona*, 384 U.S. 436 (1966), that surrounds custodial police interrogation with procedural safeguards.[5] A 6–3 majority in *Fare* v. *Michael C.*, 442 U.S. 707 (1979), held that a juvenile's request for his probation officer while undergoing interrogation was neither an invocation of his constitutional right to the presence of an attorney nor of his privilege of silence as expounded in *Miranda*. A contrary decision would have halted police interrogation of the juvenile until consultation with the probation officer could be arranged. The Court also inveighed against an expansive interpretation of *Miranda* in *North Carolina* v. *Butler*, 441 U.S. 369 (1979). Speaking for a 5–3 majority, Justice Stewart concluded that a suspect may waive his *Miranda* right to counsel during custodial interrogation, even if he has made no explicit statement to that effect.

Suppression of Evidence. The Burger Court's resistance to the exclusion of reliable evidence in criminal trials in order to deter wayward investigatory conduct[6] was manifest in *United States* v. *Caceres*, 440 U.S. 741 (1979). A 7–2 majority ruled that secretly monitored con-

---

[4] See Harris v. New York, 401 U.S. 222 (1971), and Oregon v. Haas, 420 U.S. 714 (1975) (both sanctioning impeachment use of statements elicited in violation of Miranda); Oregon v. Mathiason, 429 U.S. 492 (1977) (embracing a crabbed conception of police "custody," which triggers Miranda protections); United States v. Mandujano, 425 U.S. 564 (1976) (no Miranda rights before a grand jury); United States v. Beckwith, 425 U.S. 341 (1976) (no Miranda rights during home interrogation by Internal Revenue agents); Michigan v. Mosley, 423 U.S. 96 (1975) (permitting custodial interrogation to resume after a request to cease had been honored); Michigan v. Tucker, 417 U.S. 433 (1974) (refusing to require suppression of evidence derived from statements made without the benefit of full Miranda warnings).

[5] In the absence of substitute safeguards, Miranda requires that a suspect undergoing custodial interrogation be informed of his constitutional right to silence, that any statement he makes may be used against him, and that he has a right to the presence of an attorney, either retained or appointed. The prosecution has the burden of proving that any waiver of these rights were knowing and voluntary, an exceedingly exacting standard. See Brewer v. Williams, 430 U.S. 387 (1977).

[6] See, e.g., United States v. Peltier, 422 U.S. 531 (1975) (refusing retroactive application

versations between taxpayers and internal revenue agents may be used in criminal prosecutions if the monitoring was undertaken in good faith, albeit in violation of agency regulations. Speaking for the Court, Justice Stevens voiced fear that a suppression remedy would discourage the voluntary adoption of agency rules that curb the discretion of investigators and prosecutors. In *Baker* v. *McCollan*, 443 U.S. 137 (1979), however, the Court insisted that the failure of police to adopt reasonable procedures to detect instances of mistaken arrest did not affront constitutional safeguards against deprivation of liberty. Writing for a 6–3 majority, Justice Rehnquist stated that the Constitution is not an insurance policy against wrongful arrests and brief detentions of innocent persons.

Plea Bargaining. The Court bestowed constitutional blessing on a state policy of encouraging pleas of guilty or *nolo contendere* by offering a more lenient sentence to those who enter such pleas than they might receive after conviction by a jury. Justice White, speaking for a 6–3 majority in *Corbitt* v. *New Jersey*, 439 U.S. 212 (1978), asserted that states may extend a reasonable degree of leniency to a defendant who forgoes his right to jury trial without imposing an unconstitutional burden on the exercise of that right.

Extradition. Finally, in one of its infrequent encounters with the extradition clause, Article IV, section 2 of the Constitution, the Court held that when a neutral judicial officer of the demanding state has determined that probable cause exists to arrest a fugitive, the courts of the asylum state are powerless to reexamine the probable cause issue, *Michigan* v. *Doran*, 439 U.S. 282 (1978).

Smith v. *Maryland,* 442 U.S. 735 (1979)

Facts: At police request, a telephone company installed a pen register at its central offices to record the numbers dialed from the home telephone of a robbery suspect (Smith). The register revealed information that lead to Smith's indictment. He moved to suppress all evidence derived from the pen register on the ground that the failure to obtain a warrant for its installation violated the Fourth Amendment. The motion was denied, Smith was convicted, and a state appellate court affirmed.

---

of a decision holding roving border patrol searches unconstitutional); Stone v. Powell, 428 U.S. 465 (1976) (curtailing habeas corpus review of Fourth Amendment claims).

Question: Does the installation and use of a pen register by police constitute a "search" governed by the restrictions of the Fourth Amendment?

Decision: No. Opinion by Justice Blackmun. Vote: 5–3, Stewart, Brennan, and Marshall dissenting. Powell did not participate.

Reasons: The Fourth Amendment proscribes unreasonable "searches and seizures" initiated by the government. Its primary mission is to safeguard legitimate expectations of privacy. Ordinarily, the determination of whether government intrusion impairs legitimate privacy expectations (answerable to the Fourth Amendment) requires a twofold inquiry: whether the complaining individual subjectively sought privacy, and whether society is prepared to accept the subjective expectation of privacy as reasonable.

In this case, the questioned pen register was installed on telephone company property. It recorded the numbers dialed from Smith's home phone. Few people, however, entertain any expectation of privacy about such information. Generally speaking, telephone users realize that numbers dialed are conveyed to the telephone company for switching purposes, that facilities exist for making permanent records of the dialings, and that pen registers are employed to detect fraud, check billing, and identify the origin of obscene or unwelcome calls. Under these circumstances, we refuse to believe that telephone subscribers harbor any general expectation that the numbers they dial will remain secret.

Moreover, society would not recognize any contrary expectation as reasonable. The teaching of *United States* v. *Miller*, 425 U.S. 435 (1976), is that information voluntarily disclosed to third parties forfeits any Fourth Amendment protection against subsequent disclosure to the government. In this case, Smith voluntarily conveyed the numbers he dialed to the telephone company and revealed that information to the pen register in the ordinary course of business. In so doing, Smith assumed the risk that the company would reveal to the police the numbers he dialed.

Rakas v. *Illinois*, 439 U.S. 128 (1978)

Facts: Convictions of armed robbery were obtained against two defendants, founded in part on evidence seized by police from an automobile in which the defendants were passengers. Neither defendant claimed ownership of the automobile or the seized evidence, which consisted of a sawed-off rifle and rifle shells. A state appellate court rejected the defendants' contention that the auto search and use of the seized evidence violated their Fourth Amendment rights against unreasonable searches and seizures.

Question: Did the auto search and subsequent evidentiary use of the seized rifle and shells violate any Fourth Amendment rights of the defendants?

Decision: No. Opinion by Justice Rehnquist. Vote: 5–4, White, Brennan, Marshall, and Stevens dissenting.

Reasons: Fourth Amendment rights are personal and may not be vicariously asserted. Because the exclusionary rule's sanction against Fourth Amendment violations is so heavy-handed, it is necessary to hold to a restrictive interpretation of its protective ambit. The proper framework for evaluating Fourth Amendment claims is whether a search or seizure invaded a legitimate expectation of privacy held by the defendant. In this regard, the concept of "standing" to object to a search or seizure should be discarded because it deflects attention from the controlling expectation of privacy standard. The statement in *Jones* v. *United States,* 362 U.S. 257 (1960), that any person "legitimately on premises where a search occurs" may attack its constitutionality under the Fourth Amendment is disavowed. Legitimate presence is only one factor to be considered in applying the expectation of privacy standard.

In this case, the defendants were occupants of the searched auto. The seized rifle and shells were discovered in the glove compartment and under a car seat, areas in which a passenger ordinarily lacks any legitimate expectation of privacy. Since no special circumstances existed that might have led the defendants to expect privacy protection for themselves in these areas, their Fourth Amendment claim must be rejected.

Dalia v. *United States,* 441 U.S. 238 (1979)

Facts: Title III of the Omnibus Crime Control and Safe Streets Act of 1968 empowers courts to authorize electronic surveillance by the government in the investigation of specified crimes. Pursuant to the statute, a court approved an application to intercept, at a specified business office, all oral communications concerning a conspiracy to steal goods. Evidence obtained through the electronic surveillance was used to convict Dalia of conspiracy. The district court denied motions to suppress the evidence, despite its finding that government agents had employed covert means to install and remove a surveillance device. Although the order approving the use of electronic surveillance did not expressly authorize surreptitious entry into the designated business premises, the district court stated that such authority was implied since installation of surveillance devices without arousing the target's suspicion is otherwise generally impossible. The court of appeals affirmed the conviction.

Questions: (1) Does judicial approval of electronic surveillance and covert entry into private premises to install the necessary equipment violate either the Fourth Amendment or the Crime Control Act? (2) If such approval is permissible, must authorization for covert entry be express?

Decision: No to both questions. Opinion by Justice Powell. Vote: 5–4, Stewart, Stevens, Brennan, and Marshall dissenting in part.

Reasons: The Fourth Amendment's general proscription of unreasonable searches, the defense contends, condemns all covert entries into private premises, whether or not they are reasonable and enjoy judicial sanction. Title III of the Crime Control Act, it is argued, is unconstitutional to the extent it empowers courts to approve covert entries for the installation of electronic bugging devices. But law officers constitutionally may break and enter to execute a search warrant if other means for effectively executing the warrant are lacking. And *United States* v. *Donovan*, 429 U.S. 413 (1977), held that Title III's requirement that targets of surveillance be notified after surveillance is terminated satisfies Fourth Amendment notice standards. Accordingly, "[t]he Fourth Amendment does not prohibit *per se* a covert entry performed for the purpose of installing otherwise legal electronic bugging equipment."

It is next argued that Congress declined in Title III to empower courts to sanction covert entries to install electronic surveillance equipment. The language, structure, and history of the statute, however, demonstrate the contrary. Virtually all attempts at electronic bugging would be futile if covert entry were forbidden.

Finally, the argument is made that the Fourth Amendment prohibits covert entry to conduct surveillance approved under Title III unless the authorizing court order explicitly provides for the same. Past decisions expounding the warrant clause of the amendment, however, have discerned only three requirements: that a neutral, disinterested magistrate issue the warrant; that it be based upon probable cause to believe that evidence of crime will be discovered;

and that the things to be seized and the place to be searched be described with particularity. On the other hand, officers executing warrants retain discretion over how best to proceed with the performance of the search, subject to the overarching Fourth Amendment standard of reasonableness. Nothing in the language of the Constitution or past decisions offers a foundation for concluding otherwise. The defense insists, however, that since covert entries invade an acknowledged constitutional privacy interest independent from that impinged by the authorized electronic surveillance—security of property and personal effects—the invasion must explicitly be sanctioned in a warrant. The warrant clause would be extravagantly expanded, however, if it required courts to delineate the procedures to be followed by the executing officers whenever it was reasonably likely that Fourth Amendment rights might be affected in more than one way. More important, empty formalism would be the only beneficiary of a rule that magistrates make express what is unquestionably implicit in bugging authorizations; that covert entry may be necessary to install the surveillance equipment.

> We conclude, therefore, that the Fourth Amendment does not require that a Title III electronic surveillance order include a specific authorization to enter covertly the premises described in the order.

Brown v. Texas, 443 U.S. 47 (1979)

Facts: Detained by police in an area frequented by drug users, Brown refused to identify himself. That led to his conviction under a Texas statute that punishes a person's failure to provide his name and address to an officer "who has lawfully stopped him and requested the information." Affirming the conviction, a state appellate court rejected the contention that application of the statute to Brown offended Fourth Amendment safeguards against unreasonable seizures.

Question: Did the police detention of Brown violate the Fourth Amendment?

Decision: Yes. Unanimous opinion by Chief Justice Burger.

Reason: The contested conviction was necessarily bottomed on the view that Brown had been "lawfully stopped" by the police before refusing to identify himself. All police seizures of the person, including those involving only brief detentions short of arrest, must conform to the Fourth Amendment norm of reasonableness. The public interest in effective law enforcement must be weighed against the individual interest in forestalling arbitrary restraints on freedom in evaluating the reasonableness of particular seizures. As a safeguard against official arbitrariness, the Fourth Amendment delimits seizures to those founded on specific, objective facts that illuminate legitimate interests in detaining a particular individual, or to those undertaken pursuant to a plan embodying explicit, neutral limitations on the discretion of individual officers.

The state insists that Brown's detention was based on a reasonable, articulable suspicion that he was implicated in criminal activity. But the record discloses that Brown was detained only because he "looked suspicious" and was in a neighborhood frequented by drug users. Without any articulable basis for suspecting misconduct, "the balance between the public interest and [Brown's] right to personal security and privacy tilts in favor of freedom from police interference."

Lo-Ji Sales, Inc. v. *New York*, 442 U.S. 319 (1979)

Facts: After viewing two films purchased by a state investigator from an "adult" bookstore, a town justice issued a warrant authorizing a search of the seller's store and the seizure of other copies of the films. There was probable cause to believe, the justice concluded, that the seller's promotion of the films violated state obscenity laws. At the behest of the investigator, the justice also inserted in the warrant authority to seize any items at the store which, upon an independent examination, the justice determined were possessed in violation of state law. Thereafter, ten enforcement officials, accompanied by the town justice, conducted a sweeping six-hour search of the bookstore and arrested the store clerk. Without paying, the justice viewed scores of films shown by coin-operated projectors and ordered them seized. He also ordered the seizure of 397 magazines on display based on a cursory examination of representative samples. Finally, 431 films located behind a glass enclosure were seized on the basis of a picture visible on each film box representing the film's contents.

The seized items were the foundation for a three-count information charging the bookstore owner with violating state obscenity laws. The owner moved to suppress the items on the ground that they had been searched for and seized in disregard of Fourth Amendment safeguards that protect privacy interests. The trial judge denied the motion, and a state appellate court affirmed.

Question: Did the contested search of the bookstore and seizure of films and magazines violate the owner's privacy rights safeguarded by the Fourth Amendment?

Decision: Yes. Unanimous opinion by Chief Justice Burger.

Reasons: The search warrant flagrantly offended the particularity requirement of the Fourth Amendment by containing open-ended authority to search for and seize any items in the bookstore that the town justice deemed obscene. Moreover, at the time the sweeping search commenced, the justice lacked probable cause to believe that obscene items were located on the premises, except for copies of the two films specified in the warrant. The search, however, was not confined to these films; it was conceived and executed at the outset as coextensive with the open-ended authorization in the warrant.

The state contends that *Heller* v. *New York*, 413 U.S. 483 (1973), exonerates the search from any Fourth Amendment taint. There, the Court upheld a warrant to seize a single copy of an allegedly obscene film based on its viewing by a magistrate as a paying customer. Here, in contrast, the town justice actively participated in the police search and seizure of items. He thereby forfeited the neutrality and detachment required by the Fourth Amendment to determine the existence, *vel non*, of probable cause.

The bookstore owner's legitimate expectations of privacy were not disturbed by the questioned search and seizures, it is argued, because the town justice and police officials only occupied and viewed areas accessible to the general public. By inviting the public to enter, however, a retail store does not consent to wholesale searches and seizures that trample Fourth Amendment protections. In addition, the town justice viewed the films free, not as a paying customer, and examined the seized magazines and film boxes in a manner denied the typical patron.

> Our society is better able to tolerate the admittedly porno-graphic business of [the bookstore] than to return to the general warrant era; violations of the law must be dealt with within the framework of constitutional guarantees.

Torres v. *Puerto Rico*, 442 U.S. 465 (1979)

Facts: A Puerto Rican statute empowers police to search the luggage of any traveler arriving from the United States. Neither a warrant nor probable cause to believe evidence of crime will be discovered is required to justify the search. Invoking the statutory authority, an officer searched the baggage of an airline passenger from Miami and discovered marihuana. It was used to convict the traveler of violating the Puerto Rico Controlled Substances Act. Affirming the conviction, the Supreme Court of Puerto Rico rejected the contention that the search of the baggage offended the federal constitutional prohibition against unreasonable searches.

Question: Does the Puerto Rican statute authorizing unrestricted searches of luggage possessed by travelers from the United States violate federal constitutional safeguards against unreasonable searches?

Decision: Yes. Opinion by Chief Justice Burger. Vote: 9–0.

Reasons: The applicability of constitutional provisions to unincorporated territories turns in large measure on whether they would hamper Congress in governing such possessions. Substantial deference, therefore, should be accorded congressional views on whether the Fourth Amendment protection against unreasonable searches should extend to Puerto Rico. An affirmative answer is compelled by congressional actions over the past half century that have expressly or implicitly endorsed this territorial extension of the amendment.

Subject to a few well-delineated exceptions, the Fourth Amendment cannot countenance searches to uncover evidence of crime unless authorized by a warrant founded on probable cause. It is argued by Puerto Rican authorities that the contested statute falls within the exception for searches at the international border of the United States. That exception, however, is founded on the inherent authority of a sovereign nation to protect its territory against illegal entry of persons or goods. Puerto Rico lacks sovereign authority to prohibit entry into its territory from the United States.

The Puerto Rican statute was inspired by the growing influx of illegal firearms, explosives, and narcotics from the mainland. A generalized urgency of law enforcement, however, cannot eclipse the privacy guarantees of the Fourth Amendment.

Arkansas v. *Sanders,* 442 U.S. 753 (1979)

Facts: With probable cause to believe that a suitcase placed in the trunk of a taxi contained drugs, police stopped the vehicle and searched the suitcase without a warrant. The search revealed several pounds of marihuana, which was used as evidence to convict Sanders of unlawful possession. Reversing the conviction, the Supreme Court of Arkansas held that the trial court erred in refusing to suppress the evidence of marihuana obtained by the warrantless suitcase search. Unless there are exigent circumstances, the court held, the Fourth Amendment proscribes warrantless searches of luggage that is customarily a repository for personal effects.

Question: Was the warrantless search of the suitcase repugnant to the Fourth Amendment?

Decision: Yes. Opinion by Justice Powell. Vote: 7–2, Blackmun and Rehnquist dissenting.

Reasons: A cardinal tenet of Fourth Amendment jurisprudence generally obligates the police to obtain a warrant from a neutral magistrate before searching for evidence of crime. This obligation has been lifted only in carefully limited circumstances "where the societal costs of obtaining a warrant, such as danger to law officers or the risk of loss or destruction of evidence, outweigh the reasons for prior recourse to a neutral magistrate." Police, for example, may conduct warrantless searches of a vehicle stopped on the highway if they have probable cause to believe it contains contraband or evidence of crime. This rule acknowledges the lowered expectations of privacy associated with automobiles and the frequent impracticality of obtaining a warrant because of an auto's inherent mobility.

Warrantless searches of suitcases, however, cannot be justified on these grounds. They are commonly used to carry personal effects and create legitimate expectations of privacy. Moreover, once luggage is seized there is no danger that its contents can be altered or removed before a valid search warrant can be procured. This analysis does not lose its force simply because a suitcase is seized from an automobile.

> In sum, we hold that the warrant requirement of the Fourth Amendment applies to personal luggage taken from an automobile to the same degree it applies to such luggage in other locations. Thus, insofar as the police are entitled to search such luggage without a warrant, their actions must be justified under some exception to the warrant requirement [lacking in this case] other than that applicable to automobiles stopped on the highway.

Delaware v. Prouse, 440 U.S. 648 (1979)

Facts: A Delaware patrolman stopped an automobile to check the operator's driver's license and the registration of the car. As part of a random scheme for detecting traffic law offenders, the stop was not predicated on either probable cause or reasonable suspicion that a violation had occurred. Marihuana in plain view in the car was discovered during the stop, and one of the car's occupants was subsequently indicted for illegal drug possession. At trial, the accused moved to suppress the marihuana on the ground that the vehicle stop violated the Fourth Amendment's protection against unreasonable seizures. The trial court granted the motion, and the Delaware Supreme Court affirmed, declaring that "a random stop of a motorist in the absence of specific articulable facts which justify the stop by indicating a reasonable suspicion that a violation of law has occurred" is unconstitutional.

Question: Does the Fourth Amendment prohibit random stops of automobiles for the purpose of enforcing motor vehicle laws?

Decision: Yes. Opinion by Justice White. Vote: 8–1, Rehnquist dissenting.

Reasons: Interpretation of the Fourth Amendment is governed by a transcendent standard of reasonableness. The amendment cannot tolerate any search or seizure that is unreasonable. And the stopping of an automobile coupled with a brief detention of its occupants is a "seizure" within the amendment's protective ambit.

Privacy interests of car occupants must be weighed against law enforcement interests of the state in determining whether a random vehicle stop is reasonable. By creating substantial anxiety and inconvenience and by interfering with freedom of movement, such stops invade constitutionally cognizable privacy concerns. Random stops, furthermore, are ineffectual tools for enforcing traffic and vehicle safety laws.

> Absent some empirical data to the contrary, it must be assumed that finding an unlicensed driver among those who commit traffic violations is a much more likely event than finding an unlicensed driver by choosing randomly from the entire universe of drivers. . . . Furthermore . . . we find it difficult to believe that the unlicensed driver would not be deterred by the possibility of being involved in a traffic

CRIMINAL LAW: POLICE AND PROSECUTORS

violation or having some other experience calling for proof of his entitlement to drive but that he would be deterred by the possibility that he would be one of those chosen for a spot check.

Similarly, Delaware's enlistment of random stops to vindicate vehicle registration laws is gratuitous; statutes requiring the display of current license plates, annual safety inspection, and insurance are sufficient for this task.

> Accordingly, we hold that except in those situations in which there is at least articulable and reasonable suspicion that a motorist is unlicensed or that an automobile is not registered, or that either the vehicle or occupant is otherwise subject to seizure for violation of law, stopping an automobile and detaining the driver in order to check his driver's license are unreasonable under the Fourth Amendment. This holding does not preclude . . . States from developing methods for spot checks [such as road-block-type stops] that involve less intrusion or that do not involve the unconstrained exercise of discretion.

Dunaway v. *New York*, 442 U.S. 200 (1979)

Facts: Without the probable cause needed to make a formal arrest, detectives took a murder and robbery suspect (Dunaway) to police headquarters for custodial interrogation. After giving the warnings required by *Miranda* v. *Arizona*, 384 U.S. 436 (1966), to forestall interrogation abuses, officers elicited incriminating statements and sketches from Dunaway. At his trial for attempted robbery and felony murder, Dunaway moved to suppress this evidence on the ground that it was the harvest of police detention that assertedly violated the Fourth Amendment. After extended litigation, the motion was granted. The Fourth Amendment cannot countenance custodial interrogation predicated on less than probable cause, the trial judge declared. Moreover, the judge noted, *Brown* v. *Illinois*, 422 U.S. 590 (1975), held that *Miranda* warnings by themselves cannot purge the taint from evidence derived from an unconstitutional police seizure. Since the prosecution failed either to claim or to show that Dunaway's incriminating statements and sketches were otherwise attenuated from his illegal detention, the judge concluded, the Fourth Amendment commanded their suppression. A state appellate court reversed.

Questions: (1) Does the Fourth Amendment proscribe custodial questioning by the police in circumstances that fall short of the probable cause needed for a formal arrest? (2) Were the incriminating statements and sketches elicited from Dunaway sufficiently removed from his illegal detention to avoid suppression at trial under the Fourth Amendment's exclusionary rule?

Decision: Yes to the first question and no to the second. Opinion by Justice Brennan. Vote: 6–2, Rehnquist and Burger dissenting. Powell did not participate.

Reasons: The Fourth Amendment enshrines unyielding safeguards against unreasonable police seizures and requires that arrests be predicated on probable cause. When Dunaway was involuntarily taken to police headquarters, his liberty was sufficiently curtailed to invoke the protection of the amendment, although no formal arrest was made. The state argues that the curtailment was reasonable because Dunaway was reasonably suspected of possessing detailed knowledge of a serious unsolved crime. Past decisions expounding the Fourth Amendment, however, are irreconcilable with that argument.

In *Terry* v. *Ohio*, 392 U.S. 1 (1968), the Court concluded that in limited circumstances seizures that intrude on liberty less substantially than do arrests could be justified by less than probable cause. Specifically, *Terry* held that police could stop and frisk for weapons an individual reasonably believed to be armed and dangerous. Subsequent decisions have authorized brief and relatively nonintrusive detention of vehicles and questioning of their occupants predicated on reasonable suspicion of immigration infractions. Police detention for custodial interrogation, however, constitutes a far more grievous invasion of personal liberty than was presented in *Terry* and its progeny. To sanction such detention without probable cause would threaten to upset the Fourth Amendment balance between personal privacy and effective law enforcement. Accordingly, the seizure of Dunaway and his transportation to police headquarters for interrogation without probable cause was unconstitutional.

Incriminating evidence elicited after an illegal detention, however, is admissible at trial if the prosecution proves that its tie to the lawless conduct is sufficiently attenuated. The teaching of *Brown* v. *Illinois* in this regard is twofold: first, that *Miranda* warnings per se cannot provide the requisite attenuation; second, that the flagrancy of the official misconduct, the temporal proximity of the illegal detention and the unearthing of incriminating evidence, and the presence of intervening circumstances must all be examined to determine the attenuation issue. In this case, the incriminating evidence was elicited shortly after Dunaway's unconstitutional seizure, the interim occasioned no intervening circumstances, and the police knew probable cause was lacking for an arrest. The incriminating evidence elicited during Dunaway's custodial interrogation, therefore, was insufficiently removed from his unconstitutional detention to permit its use at trial.

Michigan v. *DeFillippo,* 443 U.S. 31 (1979)

Facts: A Detroit ordinance makes it a crime for any person reasonably suspected of criminal activity to refuse to identify himself if stopped and questioned by a police officer. Acting under the ordinance, the police arrested a suspect for refusing to identify himself and discovered a drug during an ensuing search. This led to a charge of unlawful possession. The defendant moved to suppress evidence of the incriminating drug on the ground that the arrest preceding the search was founded on an unconstitutional ordinance. The trial court denied the motion, but a state appellate court reversed and ordered suppression. Holding the ordinance unconstitutionally vague, the court declared that the arrest and search made under its auspices violated constitutional rights.

Question: Does the Fourth Amendment enjoin the suppression of evidence discovered pursuant to an arrest founded on probable cause and made in good-faith reliance on an ordinance subsequently held unconstitutional?

Decision: No. Opinion by Chief Justice Burger. Vote: 6–3, Brennan, Marshall, and Stevens dissenting.

Reasons: The Fourth Amendment offers a blanket sanction for searches made incident to arrests. The police search that yielded the incriminating drug, therefore, was beyond reproach unless the defendant's arrest under the Detroit ordinance was unconstitutional.

An arrest is valid if founded on probable cause to believe that the suspect has committed a criminal offense. In this case, the police undeniably possessed probable cause to believe the defendant had violated the ordinance by refusing to identify himself. Probable cause was not erased simply because the police lacked the prescience to foresee that the ordinance would later be invalidated by the judiciary. "Society would be ill served if its police officers took it upon themselves to determine which laws are and which are not constitutionally entitled to enforcement."

Prior decisions expounding the exclusionary rule of the Fourth Amendment have applied it to searches conducted without probable cause and without a valid warrant, even though the searches were expressly sanctioned by a statute subsequently declared unconstitutional. In contrast, the arrest in this case was founded on probable cause and was buttressed by the unconstitutional ordinance only insofar as it pertained to the facts and circumstances that constituted probable cause.

Fare v. Michael C., 442 U.S. 707 (1979)

Facts: With a history of juvenile offenses and while on probation to the juvenile court, a minor implicated in a murder was taken into police custody for interrogation. After receiving the warnings prescribed in *Miranda* v. *Arizona*, 384 U.S. 436 (1966), to safeguard the Fifth Amendment right against compulsory self-incrimination, the minor requested the presence of his probation officer. The request was denied, and thereafter the youth incriminated himself in responding to police questioning. At no time did he expressly invoke his right to an attorney during interrogation or his privilege of silence.

Charged with murder in juvenile court, the minor moved to suppress his incriminating statements on the ground that they were extracted in violation of *Miranda*. The request to see his probation officer, the minor contended, was tantamount to invoking his privilege of silence until consultation with the officer could be arranged. Denying the motion, the court concluded that an examination of all the circumstances of the interrogation revealed a knowing and voluntary waiver of the minor's Fifth Amendment rights. The California Supreme Court reversed, holding that a request for a probation officer is per se an invocation of Fifth Amendment rights that forecloses police interrogation until the request is honored.

Question: During custodial interrogation is a juvenile's request to see his probation officer per se an invocation of his Fifth Amendment rights as expounded in *Miranda?*

Decision: No. Opinion by Justice Blackmun. Vote: 5–4, Brennan, Marshall, Stevens, and Powell dissenting.

Reasons: The *Miranda* decision obligates police to cease custodial interrogation of a suspect whenever he indicates a desire to remain silent or to see an attorney. In the latter situation, interrogation may resume only after the suspect has an opportunity to confer with counsel and have him present during the questioning. This unyielding rule is based on the unique ability of a lawyer to protect the Fifth Amendment rights of an accused undergoing adversarial questioning and to forestall overreaching by the police. "Whether it is a minor or an adult who stands accused, the lawyer is the one person to whom society as a whole looks as the protector of the legal rights of that person in his dealings with the police and the courts."

A probation officer, in contrast, frequently lacks legal skills and his communications with an accused are not shielded by the attorney-client privilege. Moreover, the officer's fealty may be divided between the state and the juvenile suspect. In California, he is a peace officer and must report wrongdoing by juveniles under his supervision. In sum, a probation officer is not necessary, in the way an attorney is, to protect the legal rights of an accused. We therefore decline to hold that a request for a probation officer is equivalent to a request for an attorney under *Miranda*. In addition, there is nothing inherent in the request for a probation officer that makes it tantamount to invoking the right to remain silent.

In this case, the totality of circumstances of the minor's custodial interrogation must be examined to determine whether he made a knowing and voluntary waiver of his Fifth Amendment rights. The juvenile's age, experience, education, background, intelligence, and capacity to discern the meaning and significance of *Miranda* warnings are all relevant. The record convincingly establishes the requisite waiver needed to exonerate the minor's incriminating statements from any *Miranda* taint.

> We hold, in short, that the California Supreme Court erred in finding that a juvenile's request for his probation officer was a *per se* invocation of that juvenile's Fifth Amendment rights under *Miranda*. We conclude, rather, that whether the statements obtained during subsequent interrogation of a juvenile who has asked to see his probation officer, but who has not asked to consult an attorney or expressly asserted his right to remain silent, are admissible on the basis of waiver remains a question to be resolved on the totality of the circumstances surrounding the interrogation.

North Carolina v. *Butler,* 441 U.S. 369 (1979)

Facts: After arrest, a suspect was advised of his rights to counsel and against self-incrimination as prescribed in *Miranda* v. *Arizona,* 384

U.S. 436 (1966). The suspect affirmed that he understood his rights but declined to sign a form that would expressly waive their exercise. He then willingly answered questions and made incriminating statements without the assistance of counsel. The statements were used as evidence against the suspect in obtaining guilty verdicts on several criminal charges. The North Carolina Supreme Court reversed the convictions and ordered a new trial. The *Miranda* decision, it declared, forbids the trial use (except for impeachment purposes) of statements obtained from an arrestee under custodial interrogation in the absence of counsel, unless the right to the presence of counsel was explicitly waived.

Question: Does *Miranda* require that all waivers of the right to counsel during custodial interrogation be explicit?

Decision: No. Opinion by Justice Stewart. Vote: 5–3, Brennan, Marshall, and Stevens dissenting, Powell not participating.

Reasons: Miranda stated that a waiver of the right to counsel must be knowing and intelligent. It declined, however, to limit proof of waiver to a procrustean standard of explicitness. Although silence alone cannot prove a knowing and voluntary waiver, other evidence short of an express waiver may be sufficient. In sum, "an explicit statement of waiver is not invariably necessary to support a finding that the defendant waived the right to remain silent or the right to counsel guaranteed by the *Miranda* case." The cardinal purpose of the *Miranda* decision—to forestall interrogation that undermines a suspect's will to resist—is not thwarted by this conclusion.

United States v. Caceres, 440 U.S. 741 (1979)

Facts: The Internal Revenue Service adopted elaborate regulations to safeguard the privacy of taxpayers against unnecessary surreptitious recording of conversations with IRS investigators. Except in emergency situations, nontelephone conversations may be monitored only with the prior approval of the attorney general or specified subordinate officials in the Department of Justice. With a good-faith belief that an emergency situation existed, an IRS agent secretly monitored two conversations held with a taxpayer suspected of bribery before authorization from the Justice Department was obtained. Thereafter, the taxpayer was prosecuted for bribery and moved to suppress the recordings of the conversations because they were secured in violation of IRS regulations. The district court granted the motion, and the court of appeals affirmed.

Question: May secretly monitored conversations between taxpayers and IRS agents be used as trial evidence in criminal prosecutions if they were obtained in good faith but in violation of agency regulations?

Decision: Yes. Opinion by Justice Stevens. Vote: 7–2, Marshall and Brennan dissenting.

Reasons: Mandated neither by the Constitution nor federal law, the agency regulations involved in this case were voluntarily adopted. The unequivocal teaching of *United States* v. *White,* 401 U.S. 745 (1971), and *Lopez* v. *United States,* 373 U.S. 427 (1963), is that the Fourth Amendment offers no protection against government recording of conversations with the consent of one of the conversants. In addition, the recording of the taxpayer's conversations in violation of IRS regulations raises no due process questions. The taxpayer did not alter his conduct in reliance on the regulations and eschews any claim that the agents acted in bad faith or would not have obtained Justice Department approval for the questioned monitoring if timely application had been made.

> In view of our conclusion that none of [the taxpayer's] constitutional rights has been violated here, either by the actual recording or by the agency violation of its own regulations, our precedents enforcing the exclusionary rule to deter constitutional violations provide no support for the rule's application in this case.

In the exercise of supervisory authority, moreover, federal courts should be loath to exclude evidence secured in violation of agency regulations that have been voluntarily adopted to regularize criminal investigations. A rigid application of the exclusionary rule to every regulatory transgression would discourage executive branch efforts at circumscribing the discretion of investigators and prosecutors. Whatever power federal courts may possess to suppress evidence as a sanction for a regulatory violation, the circumstances of this case offer no cause for its exercise.

Baker v. McCollan, 443 U.S. 137 (1979)

Facts: Leonard McCollan procured a duplicate of brother Linnie's driver's license. Masquerading as Linnie, Leonard was subsequently arrested, booked, and bailed in Potter County, Texas, on narcotics charges under his brother's name. This deception precipitated the issuance of an arrest warrant erroneously naming Linnie rather than Leonard when the latter's bondsman obtained an order for his surrender. Thereafter, Linnie was stopped in Dallas for a traffic violation. A routine check disclosed the Potter County warrant naming Linnie, and he was taken into custody despite protests of mistaken identification. Dallas police contacted Potter County officials, matched the identifying information on Linnie's driver's license with that contained in the Potter County arrest records, and concluded that Linnie was the wanted fugitive. Four days later, Potter County deputies placed Linnie in a county jail, where he remained an additional four days before release. It came when officials compared Linnie's appearance against a file photograph of Leonard and recognized their error.

Linnie sued the Potter County sheriff for damages under 42 U.S. Code 1983. The sheriff's failure to establish reasonable identification procedures that would have detected Linnie's mistaken arrest, the complaint alleged, violated the constitutional protection against deprivations of liberty without due process of law. The district court entered judgment for the sheriff, but the court of appeals reversed.

Question: Did the sheriff's failure to establish reasonable identification procedures deprive Linnie of any constitutionally protected liberty interest?

Decision: No. Opinion by Justice Rehnquist. Vote: 6–3, Marshall, Stevens, and Brennan dissenting.

Reasons: Section 1983 offers a damage action to persons whose constitutional rights have been invaded under color of state law. The Fourth Amendment protects persons from arrests on less than probable cause. It is conceded, however, that Linnie's arrest pursuant to the warrant satisfied the probable cause standard. And Linnie's abbreviated detention before the police error was discovered did not offend any due process safeguard. The Constitution is not an insurance policy against the arrest of innocent persons.

> Given the requirements that arrest be made only on probable cause and that one detained be accorded a speedy trial, we do not think a sheriff executing an arrest warrant is required by the Constitution to independently investigate every claim of innocence, whether the claim is based on mistaken identity or a defense such as lack of requisite intent.

Neither is the official custodian of the accused constitutionally obligated to investigate such claims without flaw.

States may be answerable under section 1983 for detaining an arrestee for an extended period despite repeated assertions of innocence. But we are quite certain that no liability can be predicated on the type of truncated detention experienced by Linnie. State tort law may expose the sheriff to damages for false imprisonment. But a tort is not elevated to constitutional misconduct simply because a state official is the wrongdoer.

Corbitt v. New Jersey, 439 U.S. 212 (1977)

Facts: New Jersey homicide statutes offer an accused a modest incentive to avoid a jury trial by pleading *nolo contendere*. If convicted of first degree murder by a jury, the accused receives a mandatory life sentence; second degree murder is punishable by a term of up to thirty years. In contrast, a *nolo* plea to a murder charge empowers a judge to impose either a life sentence or a term of imprisonment for not more than thirty years. The sentencing provisions of the homicide statutes, therefore, encourage an accused to waive his constitutional right to jury trial in order to avoid the possibility of a mandatory life term. The New Jersey Supreme Court rejected contentions that this encouragement imposed an unconstitutional burden on the exercise of the right to jury trial and violated the equal protection clause of the Fourteenth Amendment.

Question: Are New Jersey's sentencing provisions for homicide constitutionally flawed because defendants who plead *nolo contendere* may be treated more leniently than those who are convicted after a jury trial?

Decision: No. Opinion by Justice White. Vote: 6–3, Stevens, Brennan, and Marshall dissenting.

Reasons: The teaching of *Bordenkircher* v. *Hayes,* 434 U.S. 357 (1978), is that states have a legitimate interest in encouraging guilty pleas through methods that may burden the exercise of constitutional rights or encourage their waiver. The disputed sentencing provisions reflect New Jersey's valid interest in securing *nolo* pleas as part of the plea bargaining process.

The States and the Federal Government are free to abolish guilty pleas and plea bargaining; but absent such action, as the Constitution has been construed in our cases, it is not forbidden to extend a proper degree of leniency in return for guilty pleas. New Jersey has done no more than that.

The decision in *United States* v. *Jackson*, 390 U.S. 570 (1968), which invalidated a federal statute that authorized capital punishment only for defendants convicted after a jury trial (but not after a bench trial or guilty plea), does not require overturning New Jersey's homicide statutes. The threat of death has a uniquely coercive effect on a defendant's choice regarding the exercise or waiver of the right to jury trial. Unlike the federal statute condemned in *Jackson*, however, the New Jersey homicide statutes do not reserve maximum punishment for those who insist on a jury trial; a *nolo* plea still empowers a judge to impose a maximum term of life imprisonment, the identical term mandated for those convicted by a jury of first degree murder.

New Jersey's homicide statutes are also beyond any equal protection reproach. All defendants are confronted with identical choices in the plea bargaining process. Defendants found guilty by a jury are no more "penalized" for exercising the right to jury trial than defendants who plead guilty are penalized because they forgo the chance of acquittal at trial. "Equal protection does not free those who make a bad assessment of risks or a bad choice from the consequences of their decision."

Michigan v. *Doran*, 439 U.S. 282 (1978)

Facts: An Arizona justice of the peace issued an arrest warrant for Doran after finding probable cause to believe that he had committed theft. In response to Arizona's request for extradition accompanied by the arrest warrant, the supporting affidavits, and the original criminal complaint, the Governor of Michigan issued a warrant for Doran's arrest and ordered his extradition. The Michigan Supreme Court, however, invalidated the extradition warrant on the ground that the supporting documents supplied by Arizona failed to establish probable cause that Doran had committed a crime.

Question: Once the governor of the asylum state has affirmatively acted on a requisition for extradition based on the demanding state's judicial determination that probable cause exists, may courts of the asylum state reexamine the probable cause issue?

Decision: No. Opinion by Chief Justice Burger. Vote: 9–0.

Reasons: The extradition clause of the Constitution, Article IV, section 2, commands an asylum state to deliver a fugitive to the state from which he fled upon the request of the latter's executive authority. It was intended to facilitate the speedy trial of offenders in states where alleged crimes were committed and to forestall the balkanization of justice at the expense of national unity. To encumber interstate extradition with a renewed judicial inquiry in the asylum state as to whether probable cause exists would be unfaithful to the summary character of extradition and substantially dilute its value. Accordingly, "when a neutral judicial officer of the demanding state has determined that probable cause exists, the courts of the asylum state are without power to review the determination."

Courts in the asylum state, however, may play a modest role in overseeing interstate extradition. A governor's grant of extradition is prima facie evidence that the constitutional and statutory requirements have been met. Thereafter, courts in the asylum state may review the grant in habeas corpus proceedings only to ensure that (1) the extradition documents on their face are in order, (2) the petitioner has been charged with a crime in the demanding state, (3) the petitioner is the person named in the request for extradition, and (4) the petitioner is a fugitive. These historic facts are readily verifiable.

Criminal Law: Rights of the Accused

Constitutional claims asserted on behalf of defendants in criminal actions received mixed approval this term. A striking feature of the Court's decisions was their varied deference to precedent, illuminating the wide discretion enjoyed by the justices to embrace or to disavow precedent as authority to buttress a particular decision.

The Court insisted in *Jackson* v. *Virginia*, 443 U.S. 307 (1979), that the precedent established in *In re Winship*, 397 U.S. 358 (1970), pointed inescapably to the conclusion that criminal convictions must be constitutionally overturned for insufficient evidence if a rational finder of fact could not have found proof of every element of the offense beyond a reasonable doubt. Prior to *Jackson* and *Winship*, the Court had held that a reviewing court should not invalidate a conviction for evidentiary insufficiency unless there was "no evidence" to support it. *Winship* held that due process obligated factfinders in criminal trials (and also in those juvenile delinquency proceedings occasioned by conduct that would have been criminal if committed by an adult) to employ a reasonable-doubt standard in addressing the question

47

of guilt or innocence. Justices Stevens, Burger, and Rehnquist disputed the majority's mechanical application of *Winship* to appellate or collateral review of convictions where the reasonable-doubt standard had been employed by the initial factfinder.

The decision in *Rose* v. *Mitchell*, 443 U.S. 545 (1979), witnessed another sharp dispute over the deference owed precedent. Writing for a majority, Justice Blackmun tenaciously resisted any departure from a century-old doctrine entitling defendants to attack their convictions on the ground of racial discrimination in the selection of the indicting grand jury. Justices Stewart and Rehnquist, however, objected to consecrating what they believed was unsound jurisprudence. A defendant properly convicted beyond a reasonable doubt, Stewart contended, cannot claim prejudice attributable to a constitutional infirmity in the indicting grand jury, since its mission is limited to finding probable cause. Moreover, Stewart argued, racial discrimination in the selection of grand jurors could be adequately forestalled by criminal prosecutions against wrongdoers and injunctive relief in favor of prospective black jurors. Unswayed by precedent, Stewart would have abandoned the doctrine that upsets criminal convictions to safeguard the constitutional policy of nondiscrimination in the composition of grand juries.

The cornerstone of the Court's decision in *Duren* v. *Missouri*, 439 U.S. 357 (1979), was also molded from precedent. At issue was whether a Missouri statute that empowered women to escape jury service on request deprived a criminal defendant of his Sixth Amendment right to a jury chosen from a fair cross section of the community. The Sixth Amendment, the Court had earlier proclaimed in *Taylor* v. *Louisiana*, 419 U.S. 522 (1975), cannot countenance systematic exclusion of women during the jury selection process that yields jury pools unrepresentative of the community. *Taylor* invalidated a system that yielded a 10 percent representation of women in jury pools, although 53 percent of those eligible for jury service were female. An 8–1 majority in *Duren* wielded the *Taylor* precedent to condemn the contested Missouri statute that resulted in jury venires containing 15 percent women in a community whose adult population was slightly over half female. In lonely dissent, Justice Rehnquist protested that *Taylor* dealt with virtual exclusion of women from jury service and did not ineluctably signal prohibition against jury selection systems that caused only underrepresentation of females.

A unanimous Court embraced the precedent established in *Ballew* v. *Georgia*, 534 U.S. 223 (1978), to invalidate a state law permitting nonunanimous six-person jury verdicts in criminal trials for nonpetty offenses (*Burch* v. *Louisiana*, 441 U.S. 130 [1979]). Writing for the

Court, Justice Rehnquist observed that *Ballew* interpreted the Sixth Amendment to forbid the use of five-person juries in criminal cases. The seminal teaching of *Ballew*, Rehnquist stated, was that jury deliberations would be impaired to the detriment of defendants by employing juries of such small size. The identical infirmity, Rehnquist asserted, would infect nonunanimous verdicts returned by six-person juries.

The twin precedents of *Kastiger* v. *United States*, 406 U.S. 441 (1972), and *Mincey* v. *Arizona*, 437 U.S. 285 (1978), were cited to underpin the decision in *New Jersey* v. *Portash*, 440 U.S. 450 (1979). There a 7–2 majority held that the Fifth Amendment privilege against compulsory self-incrimination prohibits the use of an accused's immunized grand jury testimony to impeach his materially inconsistent trial testimony. Speaking for the Court, Justice Stewart observed that *Kastiger* sanctified compelling testimony under a grant of immunity only if prosecuting authorities were prohibited from using the testimony in "any respect" against the witness in a criminal case. And *Mincey*, Stewart pointed out, held that due process proscribed any trial use of involuntary statements elicited from a criminal defendant. Equating testimony forthcoming under a grant of immunity with coerced testimony, Stewart reasoned that the decision in *Portash* was foreordained.

Related decisions in *Sandstrom* v. *Montana*, 442 U.S. 510 (1979), and *Ulster County Court* v. *Allen*, 442 U.S. 140 (1979), addressing the constitutionality of presumptions in criminal cases, revealed pronounced differences in the interpretation of precedent. A unanimous Court in *Sandstrom* unhesitatingly embraced the "long-settled" view that "when a case is submitted to the jury on alternative theories the unconstitutionality of any of the theories requires that the conviction be set aside." Accordingly, the Court invalidated a conviction stemming from a jury instruction regarding a presumption of intent that a rational juror might have understood as relieving the prosecution of its constitutional burden of proving every element of an offense beyond a reasonable doubt. In *Ulster County Court*, a sharply divided Court sustained a conviction assisted by a statute that permits a jury to infer from the presence of a firearm in an automobile that all of its occupants illegally possessed the weapon. Writing for a 5–4 majority, Justice Stevens insisted that precedent justified examining the constitutionality of the permissive inference on the basis of all the evidence adduced that could substantiate its rationality. Under this standard, the Court held the permissive inference unassailable as applied in the criminal trial at issue. But four dissenters, speaking through Justice Powell, maintained that precedent compelled an evaluation of the permissive inference without regard to other evidence put before the jury. Rather, Powell unsuccessfully contended, "when particular factual inferences are recommended to the jury, those factual inferences [must] be accurate reflections of what history, common sense, and experience tell us about the relations between events in our society." Applying this standard, Powell concluded that the contested inference was constitutionally flawed because common sense and experience fail to substantiate that occupants of cars containing weapons are "more likely than not" possessors of those weapons.

The decisions in *Scott* v. *Illinois,* 440 U.S. 367 (1979), and *Parker* v. *Randolph,* 442 U.S. 62 (1979), displayed a staunch resistance to following precedent. By a 5–4 margin, the Court in *Scott* held that an indigent accused is not constitutionally entitled to free trial counsel at state expense if his actual sentence is only a fine. Writing for the majority, Justice Rehnquist limited the force of *Argersinger* v. *Hamlin,* 407 U.S. 25 (1972), to mandating free trial counsel only when an indigent is actually imprisoned. Justice Brennan, speaking for the dissenters, protested that the Court's precedents, including *Argersinger,* inescapably ordained a contrary decision.

The precedent established in *Bruton* v. *United States,* 391 U.S. 123 (1968), received a crabbed construction in *Parker.* There a 5–3 majority found no constitutional objection to the admission of mutually interlocking and incriminating confessions of three nontestifying codefendants during a joint trial, if the jury was instructed to consider each confession solely against the confessing defendant. *Bruton,* in contrast, held that despite limiting jury instructions, the admission in a joint trial of the confession of a nontestifying codefendant violates the Sixth Amendment confrontation right of the other defendant, at least if the confession is "devastating" to his defense. Justice Rehnquist, writing for a plurality in *Parker,* asserted that *Bruton* offered no protection to a defendant whose own confession has gravely damaged his defense. Justice Stevens, writing for the three dissenters, maintained that the plurality had betrayed the seminal teaching of *Bruton.*

This array of criminal law decisions vividly illustrates, then, the elusive and unpredictable force of precedent in the Court's constitutional pronouncements.

Jackson v. *Virginia,* 443 U.S. 307 (1979)

Facts: Premeditation or specific intent to kill is an element of first degree murder under Virginia law. Jackson filed a federal habeas corpus petition challenging the constitutionality of his first degree murder conviction on the ground of insufficient evidence of premeditation or intent. The district court granted the petition, but the court of appeals reversed. An evidentiary attack on a state conviction in federal habeas proceedings, it declared, is of constitutional dimension and therefore may be considered only if there is "no evidence" to support it. Concluding that some evidence of premeditation had been adduced, the court of appeals denied the habeas petition. It rejected the contention that constitutional due process required that a criminal conviction rest on sufficient evidence to justify a rational trier of the facts to find guilt beyond a reasonable doubt.

Question: Does constitutional due process demand that criminal convictions rest on sufficient evidence to convince a rational trier of fact that every element of the offense had been proven beyond a reasonable doubt?

Decision: Yes. Opinion by Justice Stewart. Vote: 8–0, Powell not participating.

Reasons: The due process clause, as expounded in *In re Winship,* 397 U.S. 358 (1970), obligates the state to prove every element of a criminal offense beyond a reasonable doubt. This obligation would be hollow if convictions could stand despite the absence of evidence to convince a reasonable factfinder of guilt beyond a reasonable doubt. Accordingly, an appellate or federal habeas court must set aside a conviction if, "after viewing the evidence in the light most favorable to the prosecution, [no] rational trier of fact could have found the essential elements of the crime beyond a reasonable doubt. We reject the argument that constitutional challenges to the sufficiency of the evidence are not cognizable in federal habeas corpus proceedings."

In this case, however, a rational trier of fact could have found the requisite premeditation needed to prove first degree murder beyond a reasonable doubt. Jackson, therefore, was properly denied habeas corpus relief.

Rose v. Mitchell, 443 U.S. 545 (1979)

Facts: Charged with murder, two black defendants moved to dismiss their indictments on the ground that the foreman of the indicting grand jury had been selected in a racially discriminatory fashion. A Tennessee state trial court denied the motion, and a jury returned guilty verdicts. Seeking to overturn their convictions, the erstwhile defendants filed federal habeas corpus petitions reiterating their claim that the selection of the grand jury foreman was tainted by unconstitutional racial discrimination. The district court rejected the petition, but the court of appeals reversed.

Questions: (1) As a matter of policy, should federal courts decline (either on direct review or in habeas corpus proceedings) to entertain constitutional attacks on the racial composition of grand juries, when advanced by a defendant who has already been found guilty beyond a reasonable doubt? (2) Should such constitutional claims be denied consideration on federal habeas corpus in light of the decision in *Stone* v. *Powell,* 428 U.S. 465 (1976), which curtailed collateral review of alleged Fourth Amendment violations? (3) Did the court of appeals err in concluding that unconstitutional procedures had been employed to select the grand jury foreman?

Decision: No to questions 1 and 2 and yes to question 3. Opinion by Justice Blackmun. Vote: 5–4 on questions 1 and 2, and 7–2 on question 3, Rehnquist, Burger, Stewart, and Powell dissenting on questions 1 and 2, and White and Stevens dissenting on question 3.

Reasons: Century-old equal protection jurisprudence has permitted a defendant to challenge an otherwise lawful conviction on the ground that blacks were unconstitutionally excluded from the indicting grand jury. Dissenting in *Cassell* v. *Texas,* 339 U.S. 282 (1950), Justice Jackson urged abandonment of the rule. Any grand jury infirmity, he observed, could not prejudice a defendant who had been convicted beyond a reasonable doubt because grand juries sit only to establish probable cause. Moreover, Jackson insisted, federal criminal statutes are sufficient to deter racially discriminatory conduct in the selection of grand jurors.

The equal protection clause of the Fourteenth Amendment, however, incorporates a unique and unyielding condemnation of invidious racial discrimination. When it infects the administration of justice, the appearance of justice and public confidence in the judiciary is impaired. Moreover, invidious racial discrimination sullies fundamental tenets of a democratic society. Finally, a defendant whose conviction is overturned because of an unconstitutionally selected grand jury may be reindicted and reprosecuted. Accordingly, "we adhere to our position that discrimination in the selection of the grand jury remains a valid ground for setting aside a criminal conviction."

The state argues, nevertheless, that these attacks on the grand jury should not be considered in federal habeas corpus proceedings. It notes that *Stone* v. *Powell* sharply curtailed federal habeas jurisdiction over Fourth Amendment claims unrelated to a defendant's guilt or innocence. Alleged grand jury defects that similarly do not discredit the reliability of a conviction, the state maintains, should also not be considered in habeas proceedings. But "[f]ederal habeas review is necessary to ensure that constitutional defects in the state judiciary's grand jury selection procedure are not overlooked by the very judges who operate the system" and whose vision may be blurred by their personal and institutional involvement. Protection against racial discrimination, moreover, enjoys a unique importance in the hierarchy of constitutional values. "We therefore decline to extend the rationale of *Stone* v. *Powell* to a claim of discrimination in the selection of the grand jury that indicts the habeas petitioner." Such claims may be asserted as a foundation for federal habeas corpus relief.

In this case, however, the habeas petitioner failed to prove racial discrimination in the selection of the grand jury foreman. The evidence adduced merely showed that two former and one current foreman could not recall the selection of a black foreman for some indefinite period. But the number of foremen selected over a specified duration, a necessary predicate for inferring racial discrimination from a statistical underrepresentation of black foremen, was never established. As a matter of law, therefore, no prima facie case of constitutionally offensive racial discrimination was demonstrated in the selection of the grand jury foreman.

Duren v. *Missouri*, 439 U.S. 357 (1979).

Facts: Indicted for crimes under Missouri law, a defendant moved to quash his petit jury panel on the ground that it was selected by procedures that systematically excluded women. This exclusion, it was urged, violated the defendant's Sixth Amendment right to trial by a jury chosen from a fair cross section of the community.

Missouri offers a variety of persons exemption from jury service upon request, including all women. Although 54 percent of the adults residing in the county from which the defendant's jury was chosen were women, female representation on weekly venires during the period when the jury was selected was only about 15 percent. The defendant's jury was selected from a panel of forty-eight men and five women and was composed exclusively of men.

The trial judge denied the motion to quash, the defendant was convicted, and the Missouri Supreme Court affirmed.

Question: Does Missouri's systematic exemption of women from jury service that results in jury venires averaging less than 15 percent female violate a defendant's constitutional right to a trial by jury chosen from a fair cross section of the community?

Decision: Yes. Opinion by Justice White. Vote: 8–1, Rehnquist dissenting.

Reasons: In *Taylor* v. *Louisiana*, 419 U.S. 522 (1975), the Court held that systematic exclusion of women during the jury selection process resulting in jury pools not "reasonably representative" of the community denies a criminal defendant his right to a petit jury selected from a fair cross section of the community. *Taylor* teaches that a defendant establishes a prima facie violation of the fair-cross-section requirement by showing that the representation of a "distinctive group" on jury venires is not fair and reasonable when compared to their representation in the community, and that this underrepresentation is attributable to systematic exclusion during the jury selection process. A prima facie violation was shown in this case. Women are sufficiently numerous and different from men to qualify as a distinct group. Jury venires containing 15 percent women are not reasonably representative of adult communities with more than 50 percent female representation. And the defendant adduced proof showing that this underrepresentation persisted for a period of nearly a year and was ascribable to the exemption from jury service offered to all women.

A prima facie fair-cross-section violation, however, may be rebutted by proof that a "significant state interest" is "manifestly and primarily" advanced by those aspects of the jury selection process that disproportionately exclude distinctive groups. Missouri contends that its wholesale exemption of jury service for women was justified because of their important role in home and family life. But *Taylor* requires that this interest be advanced by selection procedures more narrowly tailored to exempting only those who in fact are burdened by family responsibilities.

> [T]he constitutional guarantee to a jury drawn from a fair cross section of the community requires that States exercise proper caution in exempting broad categories of persons from jury service . . . [However], it is unlikely that reasonable exemptions, such as those based on special hardship, incapacity, or community needs, would pose substantial

threats that the remaining pool of jurors would not be representative of the community.

Burch v. Louisiana, 441 U.S. 130 (1979)

Facts: For crimes punishable by imprisonment exceeding six months, the Louisiana Constitution authorizes trials before six-member juries, five of whom must concur to render a verdict. Convicted on two counts of exhibiting obscene motion pictures by a 5–1 jury vote and sentenced to two consecutive seven-month prison terms, Burch appealed on the ground that his conviction was unconstitutional. The Sixth Amendment right to jury trial in criminal cases, it was argued, prohibits conviction by a nonunanimous six-member jury for a nonpetty offense. Rejecting the constitutional attack, the Louisiana Supreme Court affirmed the conviction and sentence.

Question: Can the Sixth Amendment right to jury trial countenance conviction by a nonunanimous six-person jury in a state criminal trial for a nonpetty offense?

Decision: No. Opinion by Justice Rehnquist. Vote: 9–0.

Reasons: Past decisions expounding the right to jury trial in criminal cases offer no clear line marking the permissible boundaries of jury size and unanimity. In *Johnson* v. *Louisiana*, 406 U.S. 356 (1972), a verdict founded on the concurrence of nine members of a twelve-member jury was sustained. The use of five-person juries in criminal cases, however, was constitutionally condemned in *Ballew* v. *Georgia*, 435 U.S. 223 (1978). That decision was bottomed on the fear that jury deliberations would be impaired to the detriment of defendants by employing juries of such small size. For much the same reasons, nonunanimous convictions by six-member juries for nonpetty offenses cannot square with the right of jury trial. This conclusion is reinforced by the fact that all but two of the states that now have six-member juries require unanimous verdicts.

States admittedly have a substantial interest in reducing the time and expense of trying criminal cases. The use of nonunanimous six-person juries may advance this interest by reducing the number of hung juries and shortening jury deliberations. But state interests in judicial economy and expedition must yield to the jury values embraced by the Sixth Amendment.

New Jersey v. *Portash*, 440 U.S. 450 (1979)

Facts: Portash was granted immunity from criminal prosecution under a New Jersey statute for testifying before a state grand jury. Thereafter, he was indicted on the basis of evidence acquired independently from the testimony. At trial, Portash requested a ruling that, if he took the witness stand, none of his immunized grand jury testimony could be used to impeach him. The Fifth Amendment privilege against compulsory self-incrimination, he argued, required this protection against use of immunized testimony. The trial judge denied the request, Portash decided not to take the stand, and the jury returned a guilty verdict. The conviction was reversed by a state appellate court, reasoning that the trial court committed constitutional error in refusing to shield Portash from any impeachment use of his grand jury testimony.

Question: Does the Fifth Amendment privilege against compulsory self-incrimination prohibit the use of immunized grand jury testimony to impeach materially inconsistent statements made at trial?

Decision: Yes. Opinion by Justice Stewart. Vote: 7–2, Burger and Blackmun dissenting.

Reasons: In *Kastigar* v. *United States*, 406 U.S. 441 (1972), the Court declared that the Fifth Amendment forbids any prosecutorial use of immunized testimony against the immunized witness in criminal proceedings. The teaching of *Mincey* v. *Arizona*, 437 U.S. 385 (1978), moreover, is that any criminal trial use against a defendant of his involuntary or coerced statements is unconstitutional.

> Testimony given in response to a grant of legislative immunity is the essence of coerced testimony. In such cases there is no question whether physical or psychological pressures overrode the defendant's will; the witness is told to talk or face the government's coercive sanctions, notably a conviction for contempt . . . [Accordingly], a person's testimony before a grand jury under a grant of immunity cannot constitutionally be used to impeach him when he is a defendant in a later criminal trial.

Sandstrom v. *Montana*, 442 U.S. 510 (1979)

Facts: Charged with deliberate homicide, an accused admitted the killing but contended that he acted without the requisite purpose or knowledge. Instructing the jury that "[t]he law presumes that a person intends the ordinary consequences of his voluntary act," the trial judge rejected the contention that the instruction unconstitutionally relieved the prosecution of proving "purpose or knowledge" beyond a reasonable doubt. The jury returned a guilty verdict, and the Supreme Court of Montana affirmed.

Question: Did the jury instruction on the issue of intent unconstitutionally lighten the prosecution's burden of proving every element of a criminal offense beyond a reasonable doubt?

Decision: Yes. Opinion by Justice Brennan for a unanimous Court.

Reasons: Whether a jury instruction violates a constitutional right depends on how a reasonable juror could have interpreted it. In this case, the jury was told, without elaboration, that "the law presumes that a person intends the ordinary consequences of his voluntary acts." A rational juror could have construed the instruction as a command to find intent if convinced of the facts triggering the presumption. Alternatively, the juror may have interpreted the instruction as a direction to find intent upon proof of the defendant's voluntary actions, in the absence of some rebuttal evidence. That interpretation would have shifted the burden of persuasion on the element of intent to the defendant.

The due process clause of the Fourteenth Amendment, as expounded in *In re Winship*, 397 U.S. 358 (1970), and *Mullaney* v. *Wilbur*, 421 U.S. 684 (1975), obligates a state to prove every element of a criminal offense beyond a reasonable doubt. Under Montana law, purpose or knowledge is an element of the offense of deliberate homicide. The jury could have interpreted the contested instruction, however, as mandating a finding of the requisite intent if the defendant's action was voluntary and ordinarily caused death, even if the jury believed that these facts were insufficient to infer purpose or knowledge. The prosecution was thereby relieved of proving purpose or knowledge beyond a reasonable doubt.

If the jury interpreted the instruction as shifting the burden of persuasion on the element of intent to the defendant, the conviction would be similarly flawed. The unequivocal teaching of *Mullaney* is that presumptions may not be employed to alter or mitigate the state's constitutional burden of proving every element of a criminal offense beyond a reasonable doubt.

Ulster County Court v. *Allen*, 442 U.S. 140 (1979)

Facts: A New York statute permits a jury to infer that the presence of a firearm in an automobile establishes its illegal possession beyond a reasonable doubt by all occupants of the vehicle. With the aid of this permissible inference, three adult males and a young girl were convicted of illegally possessing two loaded, large handguns that were discovered in the girl's open handbag on the front seat floor of the car in which they were riding. A federal appeals court overturned the convictions of the males in a habeas corpus proceeding, holding that the permitted statutory inference was unconstitutional on its face.

Question: Was constitutional due process violated by harnessing the permissible statutory inference with other evidence to prove illegal possession of the handguns beyond a reasonable doubt?

Decision: No. Opinion by Justice Stevens. Vote: 5–4, Powell, Brennan, Stewart, and Marshall dissenting.

Reasons: The federal habeas corpus statute, 28 U.S. Code 2254, delimits the power of federal courts to entertain claims of state prisoners that their custody is constitutionally impermissible. It does not endow the federal judiciary with a roving charter to invalidate statutes that are susceptible to constitutional misuse, but as applied to particular habeas petitioners engendered no constitutional prejudice. The contested statute in this case, as expounded in the trial judge's jury instructions, merely permitted the jury to infer illegal possession of the two handguns beyond a reasonable doubt on the basis of all the evidence, including evidence showing occupancy of the defendants in the car where the handguns were discovered. The court of appeals erred in appraising the constitutionality of the statute on its face, rather than its application to the facts of this case.

Permissive statutory inferences in criminal cases survive due process scrutiny if, as applied, the inferred fact is "more likely than not" to flow from the basic fact. The evidence in this case disclosed that the incriminating handguns were too large for concealment in the young girl's handbag and were within easy reach of the three male defendants. Under these circumstances, the jury would surely be rational in inferring that each of the defendants was fully aware of the presence of the guns in the car and had both the ability and intent to exercise dominion and control over the weapons. The permissive statutory inference was exonerated of any due process infirmity since illegal possession of the handguns was more likely than not to flow from the presence of the defendants in the car when evaluated in light of other evidence.

Scott v. Illinois, 440 U.S. 367 (1979)

Facts: An Illinois statute makes theft of property valued at no more than $150 punishable by a fine of up to $500 or by imprisonment for up to one year. A convicted indigent was fined $50 under the statute, after a trial in which the state declined to provide free defense counsel. Affirming the conviction, the Illinois Supreme Court rejected the contention that the indigent's Sixth Amendment right to counsel was offended by the failure to offer trial counsel at the state's expense.

Question: Does the Sixth Amendment require the provision of free trial counsel to an indigent convicted of a crime potentially punishable by imprisonment, when the actual sentence is only a fine?

Decision: No. Opinion by Justice Rehnquist. Vote: 5–4, Brennan, Marshall, Blackmun, and Stevens dissenting.

Reasons: Whether the architects of the Sixth Amendment right to counsel contemplated any guarantee other than the right of a criminally accused to employ counsel in his defense is doubtful. In *Argersinger* v. *Hamlin*, 407 U.S. 25 (1972), nevertheless, the amendment was interpreted to require free trial counsel for any convicted indigent whose punishment includes incarceration. The linchpin of *Argersinger* was the belief that "actual imprisonment is a penalty different in kind from fines or the mere threat of imprisonment. . . ." Any extension of *Argersinger* to a broader spectrum of crimes would engender confusion, undue financial burdens on fifty quite diverse states, and bespeak infidelity to the original understanding of the right to counsel.

> We therefore hold that the Sixth and Fourteenth Amendments to the United States Constitution require only that no indigent criminal defendant be sentenced to a term of imprisonment unless the State has afforded him the right to assistance of appointed counsel in his defense.

Parker v. Randolph, 442 U.S. 62 (1979)

Facts: In *Bruton* v. *United States*, 391 U.S. 123 (1968), the Court held that the admission at a joint trial of a codefendant's damaging out-of-court confession violated the defendant's Sixth Amendment right of confrontation if the codefendant refused to testify. In such circumstances, the Court explained, a defendant lacks any opportunity to cross-examine the codefendant to discredit the adverse evidence. Relying on *Bruton*, a federal appeals court overturned the convictions of three defendants who were jointly tried and convicted of murder. None of the three took the stand, and the evidence against them consisted primarily of mutually interlocking and incriminating confessions each had made. The trial court had instructed the jury that each confession was admissible only against the confessing defendant, and was not evidence of a codefendant's guilt.

Question: Did the admission of the mutually interlocking and incriminating confessions of the three nontestifying codefendants violate the Sixth Amendment right of confrontation as expounded in *Bruton?*

Decision: No. Plurality opinion by Justice Rehnquist. Vote: 5–3, Blackmun concurring, Stevens, Brennan, and Marshall dissenting, Powell not participating.

Reasons: The *Bruton* decision was based on the fear that in some contexts jury instructions are inadequate protection against prejudicial evidence that may tip the scales in favor of conviction and yet be shielded from the test of cross-examination. Such a context, the Court declared in *Bruton*, occurs at a joint trial where the out-of-court confession of a nontestifying codefendant powerfully incriminates the defendant. Instructions to the jury to disregard the confession in considering the defendant's guilt, the *Bruton* decision maintained, could not safeguard the latter's fair trial rights that the confrontation clause was intended to secure.

When a defendant's own confession has been admitted at trial, however, a codefendant's interlocking confession will seldom, if ever, be of devastating import. The prospective benefits of cross-examining the codefendant are thus modest at best. Although a bulwark against threats to the fairness and accuracy of criminal trials, the confrontation clause generally respects the assumption that jury instructions will be scrupulously followed. When the defendant's own confession is properly before the jury, the possible prejudice resulting from the failure of the jury to follow instructions is insufficient to require departure from the general rule allowing admission of evidence with limiting instructions. Accordingly, the admission of interlocking confessions with proper limiting instructions does not violate the Sixth Amendment right of confrontation.

Employment Discrimination

Undaunted by the controversy over its pioneering foray in *Regents, University of California* v. *Bakke*,[1] examining the constitutionality of affirmative action in state medical school admissions, the Court returned this term to confront the legality of affirmative action in private employment under Title VII of the 1964 Civil Rights Act (*United Steelworkers of America* v. *Weber*, 443 U.S. 193 [1979]). As in *Bakke*, the Court's decision in *Weber* failed to set forth clear principles to guide architects of affirmative action programs.

The dispute in *Weber* stemmed from a collective-bargaining agreement between Kaiser Aluminum and the steelworkers union. It established an affirmative action plan to augment the percentage of black craftworkers in Kaiser's work force. On-the-job training programs were offered at Kaiser plants to teach production workers the skills required of craftworkers, and black employees were guaranteed 50 percent of the openings.

A white employee (Weber) was denied entry into the training program because of the 50 percent reservation for blacks. He initiated litigation attacking the racial preference under Title VII of the Civil Rights Act. Section 703 of the act makes it unlawful to "discriminate . . . because of . . . race" in admitting persons to "any program established to provide apprenticeship or other training." Accordingly, Weber maintained, his exclusion from the training program for prospective craftworkers because of race flouted the nondiscrimination norm inscribed by that section. In *McDonald* v. *Santa Fe Trail Transportation Co.*, 427 U.S. 273 (1976), Weber observed, the Court held that white employees were protected by Title VII's norm of nondiscrimination.

Writing for a 5–2 majority, Justice Brennan declared that Title VII does not condemn all voluntarily adopted affirmative action plans for private employment. He acknowledged that a plain reading of statutory terms would justify such a stance. But, Brennan insisted, legislative history incontestably evinced an intent to permit at least some types of racial preference for blacks. The Court was thus obliged,

---

[1] 438 U.S. 265 (1978). There a splintered Court concluded that a white applicant had been unlawfully denied admissions because the school reserved sixteen slots exclusively for minorities.

he stated, to disregard the ordinary meaning of Title VII. Without venturing to delineate between permissible and impermissible affirmative action programs, Brennan identified four traits of the Kaiser-Steelworkers plan that absolved it of discriminatory taint under Title VII: whites were eligible for 50 percent of the training slots; no whites were discharged and replaced by black employees; the plan was temporary, and would expire when the percentage of black skilled craftworkers approximated the percentage of blacks in the local labor force; and the plan sought to rectify conspicuous racial imbalance in an occupation that had been traditionally closed to blacks.

There are at least three flaws in Justice Brennan's opinion. Traditional canons of statutory construction,[2] repeatedly applied during the 1978–1979 term,[3] required adherence to the plain meaning of Title VII because its legislative history at a minimum disclosed congressional ambiguity over affirmative action plans.[4] Brennan, moreover, enlisted the congressional preoccupation with outlawing any government-compelled affirmative action plan to fortify the conclusion that at least some voluntarily inspired plans were not objectionable. But if voluntariness was a touchstone of the decision, Brennan is censurable for resisting any examination of the prominent government role that at least catalyzed the Kaiser-Steelworkers plan.[5] Finally, Brennan's ready imputation to Congress of a benevolent posture toward racial preference favoring blacks is at odds with the Court's constitutional assumption that blacks are especially vulnerable to the majoritarian political process.[6]

In light of the recurrent controversies that embroil affirmative action plans and the need for definitive guidance to forestall protracted and often paralyzing litigation, the *Bakke* and *Weber* decisions are remiss in pronouncing rules only for the passing hour, without offering any viable principles that can be expected to endure.

---

[2] See United States v. Rutherford, 442 U.S. 544 (1979), and In re Trans-Alaska Pipeline Cases, 436 U.S. 631 (1978) (both asserting that the ordinary meaning of statutory terms governs statutory interpretation unless it would yield an absurd result or would thwart the obvious purpose of the statute).

[3] See, e.g., United States v. Rutherford, 442 U.S. 544 (1979); Reiter v. Sonotone Corp., 442 U.S. 330 (1979); International Brotherhood of Teamsters v. Daniel, 439 U.S. 551 (1979); Touche Ross & Co. v. Redington, 442 U.S. 560 (1979).

[4] Steelworkers v. Weber, 443 U.S. 193, 219 (1979) (Rehnquist, J. dissenting).

[5] Id. at 223 and n. 2 thereon (Rehnquist, J. dissenting) (noting that the Office of Federal Contract Compliance encouraged Kaiser to adopt the contested affirmative action program).

[6] See San Antonio Independent School District v. Rodriguez, 411 U.S. 1, 28 (1973); McLaughlin v. Florida, 379 U.S. 184, 191–192 (1964); cf. United States v. Carolene Products Co. 304 U.S. 144, 152–153, n. 4 (1938).

Aliens. Aliens seeking employment in public elementary and secondary schools were rebuffed in *Ambach* v. *Norwick*, 441 U.S. 68 (1979). By a 5–4 margin, the Court sustained a statutory prohibition against hiring aliens to teach public school students if they had declined to seek naturalization. Building on the rationale of *Foley* v. *Connelie*, 435 U.S. 291 (1978), which upheld the exclusion of aliens from a state police force, the Court declared that states are entitled to discriminate against aliens in discharging important government functions. A more demanding standard of review is required if discrimination against aliens by states spreads into other areas of employment.[7]

Government Employment. Government employment also precipitated the disputes in *Vance* v. *Bradley*, 440 U.S. 93 (1979), and *New York Transit Authority* v. *Beazer*, 440 U.S. 568 (1979). In the former, an 8–1 majority perceived no due process objection to requiring participants in the Foreign Service retirement system to retire at age 60, but relieving their civil service counterparts from that requirement. In the latter, the Court ruled by a 6–3 margin that neither equal protection precepts nor the Civil Rights Act was disturbed by the blanket refusal of the New York Transit Authority to employ persons using narcotics, including participants in methadone maintenance programs.

Steelworkers v. *Weber*, 433 U.S. 193 (1979)

Facts: Pursuant to a collective-bargaining agreement, Kaiser Aluminum & Chemical Corporation adopted an affirmative action plan to augment the percentage of black craftworkers in its work force. Black craft hiring goals were set for each Kaiser plant equal to the percentage of blacks in their respective local labor forces. To meet these goals, on-the-job training programs were established at each plant to teach production workers the skills required of craftworkers. Black employees were guaranteed 50 percent of the openings in the training programs. Denied entry into a training program despite greater seniority than a black enrollee, a white employee assailed the legality of the affirmative action plan under Title VII of the 1964 Civil Rights Act. The plan discriminated against white employees on ac-

---

[7] The Court has applied strict scrutiny to state classifications that discriminate against aliens regarding welfare benefits, Graham v. Richardson, 403 U.S. 365 (1971); financial assistance for higher education, Nyquist v. Mauclet, 432 U.S. 1 (1977); admission to the bar, In re Griffiths, 413 U.S. 717 (1973); and employment in the state competitive civil service, Sugarman v. Dougall, 413 U.S. 634 (1973).

count of race, it was asserted, and therefore affronted the employment norm of nondiscrimination inscribed in Title VII. The district court held that the employment preference for blacks violated Title VII, and the court of appeals affirmed.

Question: Does Title VII forbid private employers and unions from voluntarily embracing affirmative action plans that accord limited racial preferences to blacks in order to rectify conspicuous racial imbalance in occupations from which blacks traditionally have been excluded?

Decision: No. Opinion by Justice Brennan. Vote: 5–2, Rehnquist and Burger dissenting. Stevens and Powell did not participate.

Reasons: Sections 703(a) and (d) of Title VII generally proscribe racial discrimination in hiring and in the selection of apprentices for training programs. The Court held in *McDonald* v. *Santa Fe Trail Trans. Co.*, 427 U.S. 273 (1976) that whites as well as blacks are entitled to invoke Title VII's protection against racial discrimination. A literal construction of sections 703(a) and (d) would condemn the contested affirmative action plan because it discriminated against white aspirants for the training programs on the basis of race. It is a familiar rule of statutory interpretation, however, that a thing may be within the letter of a statute and yet not within the statute, because not within its spirit nor within the intention of its makers.

The legislative history of Title VII reveals a steadfast commitment to welcoming blacks into the mainstream of the American work force. Congress was especially concerned with opening opportunities in occupations that had traditionally been closed to blacks. In addition, the legislative history of section 703(j) of Title VII discloses a preoccupation with limiting federal regulation of traditional management prerogatives over employees. By its terms, section 703(j) proscribes requiring any employer to grant preferences to rectify an imbalance in his work force. It speaks volumes, however, that section 703(j) avoids condemning voluntary racial preferences to enhance integration. "We therefore hold that Title VII's prohibition in sections 703(a) and (d) against racial discrimination does not condemn all private, voluntary, race-conscious affirmative action plans."

Several attributes of Kaiser's contested plan justify its exoneration from any Title VII taint. It opened opportunities for blacks in an occupation traditionally segregated by race. When the plan was adopted, only 1.83 percent of Kaiser's skilled craftworkers were black. In addition, no white employees were discharged under the plan, and whites could compete for 50 percent of the on-the-job training slots. Finally, the plan is temporary, scheduled to expire when the percentage of black skilled craftworkers at the Kaiser plant approximates the percentage of blacks in the local labor force. We need not decide whether other racial preference plans lacking these attributes could survive Title VII scrutiny.

Ambach v. *Norwick*, **441 U.S. 68 (1979)**

Facts: A New York statute excludes aliens from employment as teachers in public elementary and secondary schools unless they manifest an intent to apply for United States citizenship. Its constitutionality was assailed before a three-judge federal district court by aliens denied employment because they refused to seek citizenship. The district court held that the statute discriminated against aliens in violation of the equal protection clause of the Fourteenth Amendment.

Question: Is the equal protection clause violated by a state's refusal to employ as public elementary and secondary school teachers aliens who are eligible for United States citizenship but who decline to seek naturalization?

Decision: No. Opinion by Justice Powell. Vote: 5–4, Blackmun, Brennan, Marshall, and Stevens dissenting.

Reasons: The equal protection teaching of *Foley* v. *Connelie*, 435 U.S. 291 (1978), is that states may discriminate against aliens in discharging important government obligations if the discrimination is rationally founded. The operation of public schools is a paramount function of government and a primary vehicle for inculcating values necessary for a democratic political system. Both through the presentation of course materials and by example, a teacher influences the attitudes students hold toward government, the political process, and a citizen's social responsibilities. Accordingly, public school teachers fulfill a government function for which a citizenship requirement is justifiable, since it rationally furthers a legitimate state interest.

The contested statute bars from teaching only aliens who have displayed a resistance to obtaining United States citizenship. It survives equal protection scrutiny since the state could rationally conclude that such aliens are generally less qualified than citizens to impart to public school students the civic virtues and beliefs that undergird a healthy democracy.

Vance v. Bradley, 440 U.S. 93 (1979)

Facts: Section 632 of the Foreign Service Act of 1946, 22 U.S. Code 1002, requires participants in the Foreign Service retirement system to retire at age sixty. That system covers Foreign Service officers in the State Department, Foreign Service Reserve officers with unlimited tenure, career Foreign Service staff officers and employees, Foreign Service officers and career staff in the International Communications Agency, and certain employees of the Agency for International Development. In contrast, there is no mandatory retirement age for federal employees covered by the Civil Service retirement system. A three-judge federal district court held that the disparate statutory treatment of Foreign Service and Civil Service personnel regarding mandatory retirement was unconstitutional because it lacked the rationality required by the due process clause of the Fifth Amendment.

Question: Does the congressional choice to require retirement at age sixty of federal employees covered by the Foreign Service retirement system but not those covered by the Civil Service retirement system offend the due process clause?

Decision: No. Opinion by Justice White. Vote: 8–1, Marshall dissenting.

Reasons: The contested statutory distinction between Foreign Service personnel over age sixty and comparably aged federal employees burdens neither a suspect group nor a fundamental interest. Thus, the standard of strict scrutiny is inappropriate here. The varying treatment is absolved of any due process taint unless "so unrelated to the achievement of any combination of legitimate purposes that we can only conclude that the legislature's actions were irrational."

Congress imposed mandatory retirement at age sixty for Foreign Service employees to recruit and maintain exceptionally qualified younger persons by assuring that opportunities for promotion would be available despite limits on the number of positions in the service. The legitimate goal of cultivating superior achievement through early retirement was restricted to Foreign Service officers because Congress thought the importance and rigor of the tasks they performed necessitated a more insistent pursuit of excellence than that required in the government generally. This belief was sufficiently rational to protect section 632 of the Foreign Service Act from any due process challenge.

Section 632 was also designed to forestall inferior service by

Foreign Service personnel that can be ascribed to aging and to extended overseas duty under difficult and often hazardous conditions. The majority of Foreign Service officers are assigned and reassigned regularly to work abroad, and Congress acted rationally in seeking to assure that all, not just some, had the capacity for superior performance. The fact that a small percentage of Civil Service employees serve in foreign posts under conditions as arduous as those confronted by their Foreign Service counterparts does not alter this conclusion. Due process does not confine the legislative process to making distinctions absolutely congruent with primary legislative objectives. It tolerates imperfection when "rationally related to the secondary object of legislative convenience." Simply because some Foreign Service personnel may escape the rigors of overseas service that some Civil Service employees must accept does not expose section 632 to due process reproach.

It is urged, however, that section 632 is irrational because current empirical proof fails to demonstrate that conditions overseas are in fact more taxing than those in the United States or that any significant decline in mental and physical reliability begins at age sixty. This argument misconceives the nature of due process or equal protection review. So long as Congress had an arguable basis for accepting these assertions, it acted within the regime of rationality demanded by the due process clause of the Fifth Amendment. And it is futile to deny "the commonsense proposition that aging—almost by definition—inevitably wears us all down."

New York Transit Authority v. Beazer, 440 U.S. 568 (1979)

Facts: The New York Transit Authority (TA) refuses to employ persons who use narcotics, including methadone. Participants in a methadone maintenance program, designed to treat heroin addiction, brought suit attacking the legality of the TA's employment policy under Title VII of the 1964 Civil Rights Act and the equal protection clause of the Fourteenth Amendment. The district court held that the blanket exclusion of all methadone users from employment with the TA was needlessly broad and thus constitutionally infirm. The equal protection clause, it reasoned, prohibited the TA from indiscriminately denying jobs that were neither "critical" nor "safety sensitive" to methadone users who had satisfactorily performed in a maintenance program for at least one year. Noting that a disproportionate number of employees referred to TA's medical consultant for suspected violation of its drug policy and also a disproportionate number of the participants in methadone maintenance programs in New York City are black or Hispanics, the district court also condemned the wholesale employment exclusion of methadone users under Title VII of the Civil Rights Act. The exclusionary policy had a discriminatory effect against blacks and Hispanics, the district court declared, and could not be justified by any rational business purpose. Declining to reach the Title VII issue, the court of appeals affirmed the district court's equal protection holding.

Question: Does the TA's blanket exclusion of methadone users from employment violate either Title VII or the equal protection clause?

Decision: No. Opinion by Justice Stevens. Vote: 6–3, Brennan, Marshall, and White dissenting.

Reasons: Reliance on certain statistics by the district court to prove a Title VII violation was misplaced. It noted that 81 percent of employees referred to TA's medical director for suspected violation of its narcotics rule were either black or Hispanic. But this reveals nothing about the racial composition of employees suspected of methadone use. The district court also observed that 63 percent of New York City residents enrolled in public methadone maintenance are minorities. But this statistic reveals little about the proportion of minorities among TA job applicants, employees receiving methadone maintenance, or those excluded from nonsensitive jobs despite successful participation in a methadone program for more than a year. Moreover, no evidence illuminated the racial composition of enrollees in private methadone maintenance programs. Finally, the TA demonstrated that the blanket exclusion of methadone users from employment significantly advanced the twin goals of safety and efficiency. Accordingly, the district court erred in finding a violation of Title VII.

The fundamental precept of the equal protection clause is that the state must govern impartially and avoid statutory classifications inspired by animus or hostility towards any category of persons. The TA's "no drug" employment policy, embracing a total exclusion of methadone users, was the offspring of concern for safety and efficiency. The policy does not single out a class of persons characterized by some unpopular trait or affiliation that might arouse suspicion that it reflects majoritarian overreaching. Because predicting whether and when heroin addicts have been rehabilitated through a methadone treatment program involves large elements of prophecy, the TA's blanket exclusion of methadone users is neither unprincipled nor invidious. It is of no constitutional significance that the no drugs rule may deny employment to some users whose qualification to work for the TA could be demonstrated if they were individually examined.

Sex Discrimination

The Court's multiple encounters with claims of unlawful sex discrimination during the 1978–1979 term yielded a befuddling jurisprudence. The equal protection clause of the Fourteenth Amendment and the due process clause of the Fifth Amendment, the Court had proclaimed in prior terms,[1] proscribes statutory classifications founded on gender unless they are "substantially related" to the vindication of "important government objectives." This term, the Court employed this standard of review to overturn state statutes that saddled only husbands with the burden of alimony (*Orr* v. *Orr*, 440 U.S. 268 [1979]) and that barred natural fathers, but not mothers, of illegitimate children from preventing adoption of their offspring (*Caban* v. *Mohammed*, 441 U.S. 380 [1979]). A sharp retreat from this approach, however, came in *Parham* v. *Hughes*, 441 U.S. 347 (1979). There a 5–4 majority conferred constitutional benediction on a state statute that required the father, but not the mother, of an illegitimate child to have legitimated the child in order to sue for the child's wrongful death. Writing for a plurality of four, Justice Stewart asserted that gender-based classifications must surmount an exacting standard of review only if they are "invidious" or emerged from archaic sexual stereotyping. Because of unique problems associated with establishing paternity, Stewart concluded that the statutory sex discrimination was not invidious and passed constitutional muster if it was rationally founded. Finding such rationality in the statute's contribution to settlements of wrongful death litigation, Stewart declared that equal protection precepts demanded no more. Concurring in the judgment, Justice Powell employed the more exacting standard of review in exonerating the disputed sex discrimination from the asserted constitutional frailty. Four justices, nevertheless, voted to abandon this standard in favor of an indulgent standard of rationality in the absence of a prior showing of invidiousness. This division foreshadows confusing instability as the constitutional jurisprudence of sex discrimination evolves.

The Court added[2] to its past erasures of some gender classifi-

---

[1] See Craig v. Boren, 429 U.S. 190 (1976); Califano v. Webster, 430 U.S. 313 (1977).
[2] See Weinberger v. Wiesenfeld, 420 U.S. 636 (1975) (invalidating a provision that

cations in the Social Security Act. In *Califano* v.*Westcott,* 443 U.S. 76 (1979), the Court unanimously invalidated a funding provision that aided families whose fathers were unemployed but not those whose mothers were out of work. But a 7–2 majority constitutionally consecrated a host of veterans' preference statutes governing civil service employment that drastically limit female opportunities for jobs. Writing for the Court in *Massachusetts* v. *Feeney,* 442 U.S. 256 (1979), Justice Stewart observed that the disputed veteran preference statute was devoid of gender discrimination since both males and females could invoke its benefits. Voicing sympathy for the plight of most female civil service applicants, Stewart, nevertheless, refused to construe the Fourteenth Amendment as a fortification against ill-advised laws.

Sex discrimination practiced in congressional offices precipitated a constitutional controversy in *Davis* v. *Passman,* 442 U.S. 228 (1979). A congressman openly discharged a female administrative assistant because he preferred to hire a male for the post. Seeking damages, the erstwhile employee sued the congressman, claiming that her discharge offended the Fifth Amendment safeguard against sex discrimination. The suit was initially dismissed on the ground that the Fifth Amendment created no private right of action to rectify the allegedly wrongful discharge. By a 5–4 margin, the Supreme Court reversed. Speaking for the Court, Justice Brennan maintained that the Fifth Amendment presumptively endowed victims of unconstitutional sex discrimination with a private damage remedy. Only special factors, he explained, could override this presumption. Brennan noted that the speech or debate clause immunity might be asserted by the congressman as a defense to the damage suit, but insisted that it offered no justification for dismissing the complaint.

The Court encountered a reprise of *Davis* in statutory garments in *Cannon* v. *University of Chicago,* 441 U.S. 677 (1979). In dispute was whether Title IX of the Education Amendments of 1972, 20 U.S. Code 1681, by implication created private rights of action to effectuate its prohibition against sex discrimination in federally funded education programs. Answering in the affirmative, the Court nevertheless expressed consternation over the recurrent failure of Congress to inscribe its intent to confer a private right of action in explicit statutory language. These sentiments probably presage a more begrudging approach to implying statutory private rights of action.[3]

---

denied widowers, but not widows, benefits for the care of minor children based on the earnings of a deceased spouse); Califano v. Goldfarb, 430 U.S. 199 (1977) (invalidating a provision requiring widowers, but not widows, to demonstrate economic dependency as a condition to receiving survivor's benefits based on the earnings of a deceased spouse).

[3] See Touche Ross & Co. v. Redington, 442 U.S. 560 (1979) (no private right of action

Orr v. Orr, 440 U.S. 268 (1979)

Facts: Alabama alimony statutes empower judges to require husbands, but not wives, to pay alimony upon divorce. A husband obliged to pay alimony pursuant to a stipulation in a divorce decree was sued for alleged arrears in payments. As a defense, he contended that Alabama's alimony statutes were unconstitutional because only husbands are exposed to the burdens of alimony. Rejecting the defense, the trial court sustained the constitutionality of the statutes. A state appellate court affirmed.

Question: Are Alabama's alimony statutes constitutionally infirm because husbands, but not wives, may be required to pay alimony?

Decision: Yes. Opinion by Justice Brennan. Vote: 6–3, Powell, Rehnquist, and Burger dissenting.

Reasons: The teachings of *Craig* v. *Boren*, 429 U.S. 190 (1976), and *Califano* v. *Webster*, 430 U.S. 313 (1977), are twofold: first, statutory classifications founded on gender can survive equal protection scrutiny only if they are "substantially related" to the achievement of "important governmental objectives"; second, reducing the economic disparity between men and women attributable to the legacy of discrimination against the latter qualifies as an important objective. The Alabama appellate court suggested that the contested alimony statutes were conceived to aid needy spouses (using sex as a proxy for need) and also as a compensatory measure for wives exposed to discrimination during marriage that left them without skills for success in the working world following divorce. The statutes are constitutionally flawed, however, because they are not substantially related to accomplishing these objectives.

The statutes provide for individualized hearings before determining whether alimony should be awarded. Insofar as the statutes aim to aid needy spouses, the refusal to authorize alimony awards to husbands whose financial plight has been demonstrated during these hearings is gratuitous and misguided. Similarly, since individualized hearings can disclose whether either spouse was economically victimized during marriage, the compensatory purpose of Alabama's alimony statutes may be effectuated without visiting the burdens of alimony solely on husbands. Moreover, this discrimination mocks

under section 17(a) of the Securities Exchange Act); Chrysler Corp. v. Brown, 441 U.S. 281 (1979) (no private right of action under the Trade Secrets Act, 18 U.S. Code 1905).

the statutory goal of aiding financially dependent spouses. It shields from alimony obligations only financially secure wives whose husbands are in need.

> Where, as here, the State's compensatory and ameliorative purposes are as well served by a gender-neutral classification as one that gender-classifies and therefore carries with it the baggage of sexual stereotypes, the State cannot be permitted to classify on the basis of sex. And this is doubly so where the choice made by the State appears to redound—if only indirectly—to the benefit of those without need for special solicitude.

Caban v. Mohammed, 441 U.S. 380 (1979)

Facts: A New York statute requires the consent of the natural mother, but not the natural father, as a condition to the adoption of an illegitimate child. An unmarried father, whose two natural children were adopted by their natural mother and stepfather without his consent, assailed the constitutionality of the statute under the equal protection clause. To universally deny unwed fathers the same veto power over adoption as unwed mothers, it was argued, constitutes unjustifiable sex discrimination. Rejecting the argument, the New York Court of Appeals affirmed the contested adoption decree.

Question: Is the sex-based discrimination against natural fathers incorporated in New York's adoption statute repugnant to the equal protection clause?

Decision: Yes. Opinion by Justice Powell. Vote: 5–4, Stewart, Stevens, Burger, and Rehnquist dissenting.

Reasons: Statutory distinctions founded on gender can survive equal protection scrutiny only if they are substantially related to the achievement of important state objectives. The state proffers two reasons for the preferential treatment enjoyed by unwed mothers when adoption of their children is sought.

A natural mother, it is asserted, ordinarily has closer familial ties to her child than does the natural father. Even if this generalization were true as regards newborn infants, however, it becomes problematic as the age of the child increases. In this case, for example, the unwed father's display of concern and affection for his natural offspring, aged four and six at the time of adoption, was fully comparable to that shown by the unwed mother. There is no universal difference between maternal and paternal relations at every phase of a child's development that can justify the broad gender-based distinction drawn by the state's adoption statute.

It is next urged that the gender-based distinction is substantially related to the important state interest in promoting the adoption of illegitimate children. Such adoptions would be discouraged, delayed, or eliminated by the unavailability of the natural father or by his objection, it is said, if the latter's consent were made a condition of adoption. Unwed mothers, however, are as likely as unwed fathers to prevent adoption of their illegitimate children by interposing an objection. There may be greater difficulties in locating unwed fathers than mothers to procure their consent when adoption proceedings are brought, especially in the case of newborns. But where, as here, the adoption of older children is sought, the state can safeguard its interest in proceeding expeditiously by withholding veto power from fathers who have declined to participate in the rearing of their progeny. As this case reveals, a state should have little difficulty in identifying the father of an illegitimate child where paternity is admitted and a substantial relationship between the two exists. Accordingly, the discrimination between unmarried fathers and unmarried mothers in bestowing veto power over the adoption of their children is not substantially related to the state's proclaimed interest in promoting the adoption of illegitimate children.

> The effect of New York's classification is to discriminate against unwed fathers even when their identity is known and they have manifested a significant paternal interest in the child . . . [On the other hand, it] enables some alienated mothers arbitrarily to cut off the paternal rights of fathers . . . [T]his undifferentiated distinction between unwed mothers and unwed fathers . . . does not bear a substantial relationship to the State's asserted interest [and thus offends the equal protection clause.]

Parham v. *Hughes*, 441 U.S. 347 (1979)

Facts: Georgia authorizes the mother of an illegitimate child to sue for the wrongful death of that child. In contrast, a father of an illegitimate must have legitimated his child in order to bring a wrongful death action. A state court invoked the statute to dismiss a wrongful death action filed by a natural father. The father had signed the deceased child's birth certificate, had contributed to his support, had visited on a regular basis, but had failed to legitimate the child. Affirming the dismissal, the Georgia Supreme Court rejected the father's constitutional attack on the statute under the equal protection and due process clauses of the Fourteenth Amendment.

Question: Does either the equal protection or due process clause condemn the broader recovery rights enjoyed by unwed mothers than unwed fathers under Georgia's wrongful death statute?

Decision: No. Plurality opinion by Justice Stewart. Vote: 5–4, Powell concurring, White, Brennan, Marshall, and Blackmun dissenting.

Reasons: Ordinarily, a rational foundation is sufficient to sustain a state statute against equal protection attack. More exacting scrutiny is required if the statute discriminates against a class having involuntary and immutable characteristics, such as illegitimacy or gender. The contested statute, however, eschews any discrimination of this type.

No discrimination is drawn between legitimate and illegitimate children. The disputed statute simply denies a wrongful death action to a father who is responsible for conceiving an illegitimate child and who voluntarily refrains from legitimating him. The fathers are not entitled to the heightened constitutional protection enjoyed by illegitimate children, who lack any responsibility for their status at birth. The statute discriminates between unwed mothers and fathers, but without the taint of invidiousness. Under Georgia law, only a father by unilateral act can legitimate an illegitimate child. And unlike the mother of an illegitimate child, whose identity will rarely be in doubt, the identity of the father will frequently be problematic. In limiting the class of fathers but not mothers who can maintain wrongful death actions to those that have legitimated their offspring, the statute embodies a reasonable discrimination founded on gender. Accordingly, the statute survives equal protection challenge if it is rationally related to a legitimate state interest. The requisite rationality is supplied by the statute's contribution to settlements of wrongful death actions.

If paternity has not been established before the commencement of a wrongful death action, a defendant may be faced with the possibility of multiple lawsuits by individuals all claiming to be the father of the deceased child. Such uncertainty could make it difficult if not impossible for a defendant to settle a wrongful death action in many cases, since there would always exist the risk of a subsequent suit by another person claiming to be the father.

The statute deals rationally with this problem by restricting wrongful death actions to fathers whose paternity has been established by legitimating their children. The equal protection clause demands no more.

The due process challenge is built solely on *Stanley* v. *Illinois*, 405 U.S. 645 (1971), which acknowledged the constitutional interest of a natural father in raising his illegitimate children. Reliance on *Stanley*, however, is misplaced because the present case involves only the right to sue for money damages.

Califano v. *Westcott*, 443 U.S. 76 (1979)

Facts: Section 407 of the Social Security Act, 42 U.S. Code 607, offers federal funds to families in participating states whose dependent children have been deprived of parental support because of the father's unemployment. No federal funds are available to assist families when the mother becomes unemployed. A federal district court held that the statutory bias against unemployed mothers offended the constitutional protection against sex discrimination. To remedy the discrimination, the court ordered that federal funds be extended to families with needy children when either parent is unemployed.

Questions: (1) Does section 407 of the act violate the constitutional safeguards against sex discrimination? (2) Was the district court's remedial order unwarranted?

Decision: Yes to the first question and no to the second. Opinion by Justice Blackmun. Vote: 9–0 on the first question and 5–4 on the second, Powell, Burger, Rehnquist, and Stewart dissenting in part.

Reasons: The due process clause of the Fifth Amendment proscribes gender-based discrimination unless the distinction is substantially related to the achievement of an important government objective. Section 407 denies federal funds to needy families with an unemployed mother solely on the basis of gender. The deprivation affects the mother's entire family, and it is based on a statutory gender classification that triggers intensive constitutional scrutiny.

The legislative history of section 407 discloses two reasons for excluding families with unemployed mothers from eligibility: an unenlightened assumption that fathers are the financial mainstay of families and a desire to reduce costs. The assumption is a legacy of sexual stereotyping that due process cannot countenance; moreover, reducing government expenditures is not an objective that can justify discriminating against families under a gender-based classification. Accordingly, section 407 offends the equal protection standards of the due process clause of the Fifth Amendment.

Where, as here, a statute is constitutionally flawed for under-inclusiveness, two remedial alternatives are presented: nullifying the statute, thereby terminating benefits to a class Congress intended to favor; or extending statutory benefits to the class aggrieved by the exclusion. The district court properly selected the latter remedy to forestall hardships to the approximately 300,000 needy children currently receiving section 407 payments. The commissioner of the Massachusetts Department of Public Welfare, a co-defendant in this suit, insists that a more modest remedy is more appropriate. Section 407 benefits, he maintains, should be available only to families whose principal breadwinner, irrespective of sex, is unemployed. That remedy, however, would require significant restructuring of the act, forcing the district court to make a variety of policy and administrative decisions best left to the HEW secretary (who has not, in fact, contested the simpler remedy ordered by the district court here). The alternate remedy proposed by the commissioner would also have the unfortunate effect of terminating payments to current family beneficiaries whose unemployed fathers were not the principal wage earner. Moreover, states dissatisfied with the added expense of complying with the district court's remedy may withdraw their optional participation in the section 407 program. In sum, we perceive no error in the district court's effort to remove gender-bias from section 407 by simply extending its coverage.

Massachusetts v. *Feeney*, 442 U.S. 256 (1979)

Facts: Repeatedly frustrated in seeking employment in the Massachusetts classified civil service, a female applicant challenged the constitutionality of the state's veterans preference statute. It requires that all veterans (whether male or female) who qualify for the classified civil service be placed ahead of any qualifying nonveteran in the appointment process. The preference extends throughout the life of a veteran and may be invoked an unlimited number of times. A three-judge federal district court held that the veterans preference statute discriminated against women in violation of the equal protection clause of the Fourteenth Amendment. The preference is sexually discriminatory, the district court explained, because it favors a class from which women have traditionally been excluded and drastically curtails their employment opportunities. The statutory preference must have been conceived with a sexually discriminatory intent, the court insisted, because its exclusionary effects on women are so obvious.

Question: Does the Massachusetts veterans preference statute violate equal protection safeguards against sex discrimination?

Decision: No. Opinion by Justice Stewart. Vote: 7–2, Brennan and Marshall dissenting.

Reasons: The traditional justifications for veterans' hiring preference are fourfold: to reward the sacrifice of military service, to cushion the transition from military to civilian life, to encourage patriotic service, and to attract loyal and well-disciplined persons to civil service occupations. The contested Massachusetts statute originated in 1896, and has consistently embraced both females and males who have served in the armed forces. Although the beneficiaries of the statute are overwhelmingly male (98 percent), this fact is largely attributable to the exclusion of women from the military draft.

The equal protection clause offers no shield against the uneven *effects* of rationally founded statutory classifications. A more exacting justification is required of laws whose overt or covert *purpose* is to prefer males over females. The contested veterans preference statute, however, is untainted by any sexually discriminatory animus.

The district court found that the preference advances legitimate and worthy goals and was not enacted to discriminate against women. These findings dispel the contention that the preference is a pretext for gender discrimination. The fact that significant numbers of nonveteran males are disadvantaged by the statutory preference reinforces this conclusion.

A sexually discriminatory purpose may not be imputed simply because the foreseeable collateral consequence of favoring veterans over nonveterans would severely curtail the civil service employment opportunities of women. A discriminatory purpose may be established only by evidence showing the contested legislative action was conceived, at least in part, to inflict adversity on an identifiable group. In this case, no evidence suggests that the veterans preference statute was conceived to forestall the prominence of females in the civil service.

Veterans' hiring preferences represent an awkward—and, many argue, unfair—exception to the widely shared view that merit and merit alone should prevail in the employment policies of government. . . . Absolute and permanent preference . . . have always been subject to the objection that they give the veteran more than a square deal. But the Fourteenth Amendment "cannot be made a refuge from ill-advised . . . laws."

Davis v. *Passman*, 442 U.S. 228 (1979)

Facts: Congressman Otto Passman discharged a female administrative assistant because he believed that a male should occupy that position. She brought a damage suit against Passman alleging that the discharge violated the Fifth Amendment's protection from sex discrimination by the federal government. The district court dismissed the complaint. The court of appeals affirmed. The Fifth Amendment, the court stated, creates no private right of action for damages to redress injuries caused by unconstitutional gender discrimination in a congressman's employment decisions.

Question: Does the Fifth Amendment create a private damage remedy against a congressman for the injuries allegedly inflicted by unconstitutional sex discrimination in employment?

Decision: Yes. Opinion by Justice Brennan. Vote: 5–4, Burger, Powell, Stewart, and Rehnquist dissenting.

Reasons: The due process clause of the Fifth Amendment proscribes government discrimination on the basis of gender, unless the discrimination is substantially related to the achievement of important government objectives. It endows both females and males with a right to be free from illegal sex discrimination. In the absence of a textually demonstrable constitutional commitment of the issue to a coordinate political branch, the federal judiciary must enforce justiciable constitutional rights that would be otherwise unprotected. It cannot allow such rights to be reduced to hollow promises. Since the complaint alleged both a Fifth Amendment violation and the absence of nonjudicial forums to redress injury to the discharged female, a constitutionally recognized private cause of action was demonstrated.

The complaint sought damages, a traditional remedy for redressing invasions of legal rights. In *Bivens* v. *Six Unknown Agents*, 403

U.S. 388 (1971), the Court held that federal courts may award damages in appropriate circumstances to vindicate constitutional rights if there are no special factors that counsel hesitation. A damages remedy is appropriate in this case since it is easy to administer, and other forms of relief are not available. Reinstatement would be futile because Congressman Passman's tenure in office terminated in 1977.

A suit against a congressman for putatively unconstitutional actions taken in the course of his official conduct raises special concerns counselling caution. We hold, however, that these concerns are coextensive with the judicial immunity offered legislators by the speech or debate clause of the Constitution, Article I, Section 6, clause 1. This immunity may be asserted as a defense on remand. But if it is unavailing, Passman should be held answerable to the law as are ordinary persons.

Although Congress has tenaciously refused to offer statutory protection against sex discrimination to its employees not hired through the competitive service, it has voiced no explicit declaration that money damages should be denied for unconstitutional discrimination in employment. The court of appeals, nevertheless, was reluctant to embrace a damage remedy for fear that it would precipitate a deluge of similar suits. Conservation of scarce judicial resources, however, is no excuse for discarding sound constitutional principles.

Cannon v. *University of Chicago*, 441 U.S. 677 (1979)

Facts: Denied admission to two private medical schools, a female applicant brought suit under Title IX of the Education Amendments of 1972, 20 U.S. Code 1681, alleging that her rejections were unlawfully founded on gender. Section 1681 prohibits sex discrimination in any education program or activity subsidized by federal funds. The district court dismissed the complaint, holding that section 1681 neither expressly nor impliedly creates a private remedy to redress unlawful sex discrimination. The court of appeals affirmed, declaring that the sole remedy for violation of section 1681 was the termination of federal financial support after an agency hearing pursuant to 20 U.S. Code 1682.

Question: Does section 1681 create a private right of action to effectuate its prohibition against sex discrimination?

Decision: Yes. Opinion by Justice Stevens. Vote: 6–3, White, Blackmun, and Powell dissenting.

Reasons: As explained in *Cort* v. *Ash*, 442 U.S. 66 (1975), four factors must be carefully analyzed to determine whether Congress by implication created a private right of action to redress violations of a federal statute: whether the plaintiff belongs to a class for whose especial benefit the statute was enacted, whether legislative history discloses an intent to create a private remedy, whether a private remedy for the plaintiff would disturb any underlying legislative purpose, and whether state law has been the traditional source for regulating the allegedly unlawful conduct.

The express language of a statute answers the question of whether its enactment was for the benefit of a special class that includes the plaintiff. The explicit command of section 1681 is that "[n]o person" shall be victimized by sex discrimination in federally assisted education programs. Individuals are expressly identified as the beneficiary class protected by the statute, which counsels in favor of implying a private cause of action.

The legislative history of Title IX reinforces that conclusion, since it plainly indicates that Congress intended to create a private remedy for Title IX infractions.

A private remedy would also be faithful to the twin purposes of Title IX: proscribing the use of federal resources to support discriminatory practices, and protecting individuals against those practices. The first purpose is achieved by terminating federal funds for institutions engaged in discriminatory practices. That remedy, however, may be inappropriate for isolated incidents of discrimination. As a practical matter, moreover, the primary federal enforcement agency lacks the resources to investigate all Title IX complaints and would welcome the assistance that individual lawsuits would bring in furthering the nondiscrimination policy of Title IX. A private cause of action and the award of individual relief under section 1681 is thus fully consistent with—and in some cases necessary for—the orderly enforcement of Title IX.

Finally, since the Civil War, the federal government and the federal courts have been the primary sanctuary for individual victims of invidious discrimination of any sort, including gender-based discrimination. In addition, the expenditure of federal funds triggers application of section 1681. That section, therefore, avoids regulation of conduct traditionally addressed by state law.

In sum, each of the factors identified in *Cort* favor implication of a cause of action for private victims of sex discrimination. We admonish Congress, however, that when it intends to entrust private parties with a cause of action to support their statutory rights, the preferred course is to voice that intent explicitly when it creates those rights.

Freedom of Speech and Press

Culminating with its harshly criticized decision in *Gannett Company, Inc.* v. *DePasquale*, 443 U.S. 368 (1979), endorsing secret pretrial suppression hearings, the Court handed the press a trilogy of bitter defeats during the 1978–1979 term. A 5–4 majority in *Gannett* declared that the accused, but not members of the public, may insist on a public trial in criminal cases under the Sixth Amendment. Writing for the Court, Justice Stewart acknowledged several weighty interests promoted by public trials: deterring perjured or inaccurate testimony, inducing undiscovered witnesses to offer relevant evidence, encouraging rectitude and conscientious performance by trial participants, and educating the public about the judicial process. He maintained, nevertheless, that when both the prosecutor and judge accede to a defendant's request to close a pretrial suppression hearing, these interests are still adequately safeguarded.

Stewart also noted that the trial judge granted the motion to close the pretrial suppression hearing under the following circumstances: neither the prosecutor nor court spectators interposed any immediate objection; the press was offered a belated opportunity to oppose closure; closure was ordered only after a judicial finding that an open hearing would create a "reasonable probability" of trial prejudice to the defendants; and once this danger had passed, a transcript of the suppression hearing was released. Any putative constitutional protection afforded the press to attend pretrial hearings, Stewart asserted, must yield, at least in this case, to the defendants' right to a fair trial.

The *Gannett* decision is vulnerable to criticism on at least two counts. It contravenes Stewart's previous assertion that the architects of the First Amendment envisioned a free press as a deterrent to official wrongdoing by providing "organized expert scrutiny of government."[1] Experience offers no foundation for Stewart's blithe assumption that prosecutors and judges are so beyond temptation that they would never connive with an accused to close a pretrial hearing for ulterior and illegitimate reasons. The press cannot carry out its constitutional mission and deter such misconduct without access to

---

[1] Address of Potter Stewart, "Or of the Press," Yale Law School Sesquicentennial Convocation, New Haven, Connecticut, November 2, 1974.

the hearing. And since a formidable judicial arsenal, delineated in *Nebraska Press Ass'n.* v. *Stuart*,[2] may be employed to offset the potentially prejudicial effects of pretrial publicity, there would still seem to be sufficient protection for the defendants' right to a fair trial even with an open suppression hearing.

The majority of trial judges, moreover, are inclined, much as anyone else, to embrace measures that make their jobs easier. Closing pretrial suppression hearings eases the burden of jury selection. Most trial judges will thus be reflexively disposed to favoring closure while discounting the significant public interests advanced by press scrutiny. The Court's cheerful assumption that trial judges will scrupulously defend these interests is unsound, a view substantiated by the flurry of trial court decisions in the wake of *Gannett* barring the press and public from pretrial and sentencing hearings as well as from actual trials.[3]

The so-called actual malice rule set out in *New York Times* v. *Sullivan* in 1964[4] that shields the news media from defamation suits initiated by public officials or public figures was central to three decisions inimical to free press interests. Derived from First Amendment considerations, the actual malice rule bars defamation recoveries against the media in lawsuits brought by public officials[5] or "public figures," when there is no proof that a damaging falsehood was published with knowledge of its falsity or with reckless disregard of whether it was false or not. In *Herbert* v. *Lando*, 441 U.S. 153 (1979), a 6–3 majority repudiated the claim by media personnel that they enjoy a First Amendment immunity from answering questions by defamation plaintiffs inquiring into their state of mind or into their editorial process in order to prove "actual malice."

In two cases, the Court circumscribed the "public figure" status that makes it necessary to prove "actual malice" by defendants. The narrower the definition, the greater the liability exposure of the media,

---

[2] 427 U.S. 539 (1976). The Court noted that a change of trial venue, postponement of the trial, extensive questioning of prospective jurors to screen out those with bias, sequestration of jurors, and injunctions prohibiting attorneys, parties, and witnesses from making extrajudicial statements that disclose prejudicial information could all be employed to rectify or mitigate the effects of pretrial publicity.

[3] See *Washington Post*, A6, August 5, 1979.

[4] 376 U.S. 254 (1964).

[5] The concept of a public official remains cloudy. It has been held to embrace an elected city commissioner of public affairs, New York Times v. Sullivan, supra, n. 4; elected municipal judges, Garrison v. Louisiana, 379 U.S. 64 (1964); a deputy sheriff, St. Amant v. Thompson, 39 U.S 727 (1968); and a candidate for the Senate, Monitor Patriot Co. v. Roy, 401 U.S. 265 (1971).

since private persons unlike "public figures," may recover for defamatory falsehoods published by the media upon a mere showing of negligence.[6] Justice Rehnquist, writing for an 8–1 majority in *Wolston v. Reader's Digest Ass'n., Inc.*, 443 U.S. 157 (1979), declared that persons convicted of criminal conduct are not automatically converted to public figures for purposes of comment on issues relating to their convictions. And simply because a citizen is a recipient of government grants, Chief Justice Burger declared for the Court in *Hutchinson v. Proxmire*, 443 U.S. 111 (1979), is not enough to make him a public figure.

Free press and speech interests prevailed in *Smith v. Daily Mail Publishing Co.*, 443 U.S. 97 (1979) and *Givhan v. Western Line Consolidated School District*, 439 U.S. 410 (1979). In the former, the Court voted 8–0 to invalidate the indictment of two newspapers for publishing the names of alleged juvenile offenders. In the latter, a unanimous Court declared that the First Amendment protects the expression of views communicated in private as well as in public.

Finally, the Court signaled a retreat from the commercial speech doctrine expounded in *Bates v. State Bar of Arizona*,[7] *Linmark Associates v. Willingboro*,[8] and *Virginia State Board of Pharmacy v. Virginia Citizens Consumer Council*.[9] By a 7–2 margin in *Friedman v. Rogers*, 440 U.S. 1 (1979), the Court held that a state ban on the practice of optometry under a trade name did not violate the First Amendment. Writing for the majority, Justice Powell acknowledged that a trade name could be employed to identify an optometrical practice and to convey information about the type, price, and quality of the service offered in that practice. Intelligent consumer choices are clearly facilitated by the truthful use of trade names. Powell maintained, nevertheless, that the state's paternalistic interest in shielding the public from deceptive use of trade names justified a wholesale prohibition. That conclusion, however, betrays the spirit of *Bates*,[10] *Linmark Associates*,[11] and *Virginia Citizens Consumer Council*,[12] all of which denied the legitimacy of a paternalistic approach to the regulation of truthful commercial information.

---

[6] See Gertz v. Welch, Inc., 418 U.S. 323 (1974).

[7] 433 U.S. 350 (1977) (invalidating a ban on newspaper advertisement of prices for routine legal services).

[8] 431 U.S. 85 (1977) (invalidating a ban on posting "For Sale" signs on homes).

[9] 425 U.S. 748 (1975) (invalidating a ban on price advertising for prescription drugs).

[10] See n. 7, supra, at 374–375.

[11] See n. 8, supra, at 96–97.

[12] See n. 9, supra, at 766–770.

Gannett Company, Inc. v. DePasquale, 443 U.S. 368 (1979)

Facts: A homicide in Seneca County, New York, elicited newspaper publicity about police efforts that resulted in the arrest of two suspects and led to their indictment for murder by a Seneca County grand jury. The defendants made pretrial motions to suppress statements and evidence that were allegedly the fruits of involuntary confessions. Voicing concern that adverse publicity had jeopardized their rights to a fair trial, the defendants also moved to exclude the public and the press from the suppression hearing. Hearing no objection from either the prosecuting attorney or a reporter present in the courtroom, the trial judge granted the motion.

The following day, however, the reporter asserted a constitutional right to attend the hearing and to receive immediate access to the transcript. Although the hearing had terminated, the trial judge scheduled a full briefing on the requests. After considering the submissions of the interested parties, the judge declared that both the exclusion order and denial of immediate access to the transcript were constitutionally unassailable. Although the First Amendment endows the press with some right of access to pretrial judicial proceedings, the judge acknowledged, it must yield to a defendant's right to a fair trial when access would pose a "reasonable probability" of trial prejudice. In this case, the judge concluded, opening the suppression hearing would expose adverse information, excludable at trial, and thus would threaten the defendants' right to an impartial petit jury. The New York Court of Appeals affirmed.

Question: Does either the Sixth Amendment's guarantee of public trials in criminal cases or the First Amendment's protection of a free press proscribe a trial judge, with the consent of the accused and the prosecutor, from closing a pretrial suppression hearing in order to assure a fair trial?

Decision: No. Opinion by Justice Stewart. Vote: 5–4, Blackmun, Brennan, White, and Marshall dissenting.

Reasons: The Sixth Amendment provides that "[i]n all criminal prosecutions, the accused shall enjoy the right of a . . . public trial. . . ." It speaks volumes, however, that the Constitution omits endowing the public with an express right of access to a criminal trial. Both the history of the public trial guarantee and its exposition in prior decisions compel the conclusion that its sole beneficiary is the accused. Members of the public lack any Sixth Amendment right to insist upon a public trial.

Although a defendant may insist on a public trial under the Sixth Amendment, the amendment offers no correlative absolute right to compel a private trial. Important interests of society are advanced by public trials: forestalling perjured or inaccurate testimony, inducing undiscovered witnesses to offer relevant evidence, encouraging trial participants to perform conscientiously, and educating the public about the operations of the judicial system. These interests, however, are adequately safeguarded when both the prosecutor and the trial judge concur with the accused in the need to close a pretrial suppression hearing.

The plaintiff asserts, nevertheless, that the First Amendment entitles members of the press and the public to attend pretrial suppression hearings. Even assuming this putative right exists in some circumstances, it was subservient in this case to the accused's right to a fair trial. This conclusion is founded on the following facts: the defendants' closure motion was greeted with silence by court spectators; the trial judge offered the press a belated but full opportunity to argue against closure; closure was ordered only after a careful finding that an open proceeding would create a "reasonable probability" of trial prejudice to the defendants, and once this danger has dissipated, a transcript of the suppression hearing was released. Under these circumstances, no right of the press to attend criminal trials was violated.

Herbert v. *Lando,* 441 U.S. 153 (1979)

Facts: Anthony Herbert, an army officer with wartime service in Vietnam, attracted widespread media attention when he accused his superior officers of concealing reports of atrocities and other war crimes. Herbert and his accusations were featured on the CBS program "60 Minutes," produced by Barry Lando and narrated by Mike Wallace. Lando later published a related article in the *Atlantic Monthly* magazine.

Herbert sued Lando, Wallace, CBS, and the *Atlantic Monthly* for defamation, alleging that the program and article falsely and maliciously portrayed him as a liar who had fabricated war-crimes charges to explain why he had been relieved of command. Since Herbert concededly was a "public figure," the First Amendment's protection of the media, as expounded in *New York Times* v. *Sullivan,* 376 U.S.

254 (1964), and *Curtis Publishing Co.* v. *Butts,* 388 U.S. 130 (1967), precluded any recovery, unless there was proof that the defendants had published a damaging falsehood with "actual malice"—that is, with knowledge of the falsehood or with reckless disregard of whether it was false or not. Reckless disregard, as the Court declared in *St. Amant* v. *Thompson,* 390 U.S. 727 (1968), can be established only if the defendant subjectively entertained serious doubts as to the truth of the matters published. Such subjective awareness, the Court declared in *Gertz* v. *Robert Welch, Inc.,* 418 U.S. 323 (1974), can be inferred if there are obvious reasons to suspect the veracity of the informant or the accuracy of his reports.

Seeking evidence of "actual malice" during pretrial discovery, Herbert propounded a series of questions to Lando about his belief in the veracity of persons interviewed and about the editorial process used in preparing the broadcast in question. Refusing to answer, Lando argued that the First Amendment foreclosed inquiry into such matters. The district court rejected the claim of constitutional privilege, but the court of appeals reversed. The constitutional protection of a free press, it declared, shielded Lando from any inquiry about his thoughts, opinions, and conclusions respecting material gathered by him and about his conversations with editorial colleagues.

Question: In seeking evidence of "actual malice" to support a defamation suit, is a plaintiff barred by the First Amendment from demanding that media representatives answer questions about their state of mind and the editorial process antedating the contested broadcast?

Answer: No. Opinion by Justice White. Vote: 6–3, Brennan, Stewart, and Marshall dissenting.

Reasons: Nothing in *New York Times* and its progeny established or presaged any First Amendment foundation for circumscribing the sources of evidence available to a defamation plaintiff to prove the elements of his case. Proof of actual malice ineluctably focuses inquiry on the state of mind and the editorial processes of the alleged defamer. Without such inquiries, public officials and public figures would face insurmountable barriers in seeking to satisfy the *New York Times* actual malice rule.

The defendants maintain, nevertheless, that a First Amendment haven should be created to shield inquiry into the thoughts, opinions, and conclusions of the broadcasters. Otherwise, they say, the inhibiting effects on the editorial process and editorial decision making will be intolerable. A defamation plaintiff, it is contended, could still resort to objective evidence to prove actual malice.

To rule out direct inquiry into the state of mind and editorial processes of alleged media defamers, however, might make it impossible to obtain critical evidence of malice. To permit such inquiry may inhibit editorial decision making for fear of disseminating knowing or reckless falsehoods. But the malicious dissemination of false information lacks any constitutional virtue; thus editorial inhibitions that restrain the publication of such falsehoods are not offensive to First Amendment values.

> [W]e find it difficult to believe that error-avoiding procedures will be terminated or stifled simply because there is liability for culpable error and because the editorial process will itself be examined in the tiny percentage of instances in which error is claimed and litigation ensues. Nor is there sound reason to believe that editorial exchanges and the editorial process are so subject to distortion that they should be immune from examination in order to avoid erroneous judgments in defamation suits.

Evidentiary privileges in litigation are disfavored, since they impede the search for the truth. To proscribe relevant inquiries into the state of mind and editorial process of an alleged defamer would betray this principle and make no contribution to First Amendment goals. We decline, therefore, to invest any such proscription with constitutional status.

Wolston v. *Reader's Digest Association, Inc.,* **443 U.S. 157 (1979)**

Facts: In 1974, the Reader's Digest published a book (*KGB*) chronicling Russian espionage activity. It contained assertions that Ilya Wolston had been identified as a Soviet agent in the United States and had been indicted for espionage. Wolston had not in fact been indicted for espionage, though he had received a criminal contempt citation for failing to answer the subpoena of a grand jury espionage probe in 1958. He therefore brought suit against the author and publishers of *KGB* alleging that the assertions were false and defamatory. The district court granted summary judgment for the defendants. It explained that Wolston was a "public figure" and that the First Amendment therefore shielded the defendants from damages, in the absence of any proof that the alleged defamatory falsehoods had been published with "actual malice." The court of appeals affirmed.

Question: Was Wolston a "public figure," whose right to recover for the alleged defamatory falsehoods was circumscribed under the First Amendment by an actual malice requirement?

Decision: No. Opinion by Justice Rehnquist. Vote: 8–1, Brennan dissenting.

Reasons: In *New York Times* v. *Sullivan*, 376 U.S. 254 (1964), the Court held that the First Amendment prohibits a public official from recovering damages for a defamatory falsehood relating to his official conduct, unless there is proof that the statement was made with "actual malice"—that is, with knowledge that it was false or with reckless disregard of whether it was false or not. The actual malice limitation on defamation recoveries was extended to "public figures" in *Curtis Publishing Co.* v. *Butts*, 388 U.S. 130 (1967). The attributes of "public figures" were expounded in *Gertz* v. *Robert Welch, Inc.*, 418 U.S. 323 (1974). This status may be acquired, the Court explained, either by assuming a role of special prominence in the affairs of society or by voluntarily seeking a prominent position in the resolution of particular public controversies. Although persons in the former category are public figures for all purposes, the latter are so only with respect to statements concerning the public controversy that precipitated their voluntary action.

The defendant claims that Wolston falls within the second category of public figures because of a 1958 contempt citation stemming from a grand jury inquiry into Soviet espionage. Wolston's involvement in the controversy swirling over Soviet espionage, however, lacked the critical element of voluntariness. Only his refusal to respond to a grand jury subpoena led to the contempt citation and the media attention. Wolston eschewed any attempt to arouse public sentiment in his favor, against the espionage investigation, or behind any other issue of public concern. He passively accepted the contempt citation and steadfastly sought a private life thereafter. Accordingly, Wolston was not a public figure for purposes of public commentary on Soviet intelligence. We unequivocally disavow the view "that any person who engages in criminal conduct automatically becomes a public figure for purposes of comment on a limited range of issues relating to his conviction."

Hutchinson v. Proxmire, 443 U.S. 111 (1979)

Facts: To publicize and discredit what he perceived as examples of outlandishly wasteful government expenditures, Senator William

Proxmire initiated a "Golden Fleece of the Month Award." Three government agencies received one such award for funding research undertaken by Hutchinson to explore objective measures of animal aggression. A press release and newsletters to constituents were issued by the senator to publicize the award and to cast obloquy on Hutchinson's research. Hutchinson brought action against the senator alleging that the press release and newsletter contained false charges that injured his professional standing and inflicted mental and physical distress. Granting summary judgment for the senator, the district court declared that the speech or debate clause (Article I, Section 6, clause 1 of the Constitution) afforded absolute immunity for the publicity associated with the Golden Fleece award. The district court stated that Hutchinson was a "public figure" whose rights of recovery for defamatory statements are circumscribed by the First Amendment. A public figure is constitutionally bound to prove that a false statement was published with "actual malice" as a foundation for any recovery, the district court noted, but evidence of the requisite malice was lacking. The court of appeals affirmed.

Questions: (1) Did the speech or debate clause shield the senator from Hutchinson's suit founded on publicity about the senator's Golden Fleece Award contained in his press release and newsletters? (2) Was Hutchinson a "public figure" required by the First Amendment to prove "actual malice" as a predicate for redressing injuries attributable to false statements of fact?

Decision: No to both questions. Opinion by Chief Justice Burger. Vote: 8–1, Brennan dissenting.

Reasons: The speech or debate clause bars judicial inquiry into the legislative acts of senators or congressmen. Legislative acts embrace activity that is an integral part of the deliberative and communicative processes in which members of Congress participate. The immunity shield of the clause is delimited by what is necessary to preserve the integrity of the legislative process.

In *Gravel* v. *United States*, 408 U.S. 606 (1972), and *Doe* v. *McMillan*, 412 U.S. 306 (1973), the Court declared that the private publication or republication of statements made in the course of legislative activity fall outside the protective umbrella of the speech or debate clause. The Court maintained that public dissemination of such statements is not essential to the deliberative functions of Congress. These precedents compel the conclusion that Senator Proxmire's press release and newsletters containing allegedly false statements about Hutchinson were not legislative acts and thus were not protected by the clause. Newsletters and press releases may be effective and important vehicles for informing the public about legislative matters and catching the attention of congressional colleagues. But that is not sufficient reason to confer speech or debate immunity.

As expounded in *Curtis Publishing Co.* v. *Butts*, 388 U.S. 130 (1968), the First Amendment prohibits "public figures" from recovering damages for defamatory falsehoods, unless there is proof that the statements were published with "actual malice"—that is, with knowledge of their falsity or with reckless disregard of whether they were false or not. Ordinarily, as the Court explained in *Gertz* v. *Robert Welch, Inc.*, 418 U.S. 323 (1974), a public figure is one who has thrust himself to the forefront of a particular public controversy in order to influence its resolution. The court of appeals reasoned that Hutchinson was a public figure for the purpose of comment on his federally funded research. But the researcher declined to inject himself into any public controversy about the government grants Senator Proxmire assailed by his Golden Fleece award, and he eschewed attempts to sway public opinion. Hutchinson shunned any prominent role in the public dialogue about the wisdom of federal grants generally. Finally, he lacked the regular and continuing access to the media that is a prime attribute of a public figure. A private citizen should not be crowned with the status of a public figure simply because he receives government grants.

Smith v. *Daily Mail Publishing Co.*, 443 U.S. 97 (1979)

Facts: A West Virginia statute makes it a crime for newspapers, but not the broadcast media, to publish the name of an accused juvenile offender without the written approval of the juvenile court. Reporters for two newspapers obtained the name of a fourteen-year-old youth arrested in the wake of a killing by questioning witnesses, the police, and an assistant prosecuting attorney. Thereafter, the newspapers were indicted for publishing the youth's name, although it was lawfully broadcast concurrently by three radio stations. The West Virginia Supreme Court dismissed the indictment, reasoning that its statutory foundation violated the free press tenets of the First Amendment.

Question: Does the West Virginia statute proscribing the publication of the names of alleged juvenile offenders by newspapers without court approval violate the First Amendment?

Decision: Yes. Opinion by Chief Justice Burger. Vote: 8–0, Powell not participating.

Reasons: The free press guarantee of the First Amendment prohibits the punishment of newspapers for publishing lawfully obtained truthful information of public significance "absent a need to further a state interest of the highest order." Protecting the anonymity of the juvenile offender is the sole interest advanced by the contested statute. Anonymity, it is said, is necessary to forestall the social stigma and loss of employment opportunities that publication would bring. This interest in juvenile rehabilitation is not sufficient to justify criminally punishing newspapers that publish the name of an alleged offender that was discovered through lawful means. The statutory penalty is unreasonable since the electronic media may identify suspected juvenile offenders without penalty. The confidentiality of juvenile proceedings can be adequately safeguarded by prohibiting participants from disclosing the names of involved youths to nonparticipants. In sum, the state interest assertedly advanced by the questioned statute in this case could not justify inflicting criminal penalties on the newspapers.

Givhan v. *Western Line Consolidated School District*, 439 U.S. 410 (1979)

Facts: Seeking reinstatement, a former public school teacher brought suit against a school district alleging that its decision not to renew her contract infringed her First Amendment right of free speech. Granting the requested relief, a federal district court found that the nonrenewal decision was constitutionally tainted because it was primarily bottomed on the teacher's criticisms of the district's policies and practices voiced in private encounters with a school principal. The court of appeals reversed, holding that private as opposed to public expression by government employees falls outside the protection of the First Amendment.

Question: Do government employees forfeit First Amendment protection for the expression of views if they communicate them in private rather than in public?

Decision: No. Opinion by Justice Rehnquist. Vote: 9–0.

Reasons: The First Amendment enjoins the government from abridging freedom of speech.

Neither the Amendment itself nor our decisions indicate that this freedom is lost to the public employee who arranges to communicate privately with his employer rather than to spread his views before the public. We decline to adopt such a view of the First Amendment.

Friedman v. *Rogers*, 440 U.S. 1 (1979)

Facts: A "commercial" optometrist brought suit against several members of the Texas Optometry Board seeking to overturn two statutes that allegedly curtailed his ability to compete with "professional" optometrists. The first prohibits the practice of optometry under a trade name. The second commands that four of the board's six members, charged with enforcing the 1969 Texas Optometry Act, belong to the Texas Optometric Association (TOA), an organization of professional optometrists. The organization excludes commercial optometrists because their business methods are inconsistent with the code of ethics of the American Optometric Association.

The prohibition against the use of trade names, the plaintiff claimed, violated the First Amendment's protection of truthful commercial speech; and reserving four of the six board seats to members of the TOA assertedly violated the equal protection clause of the Fourteenth Amendment.

The district court invalidated the ban on trade names as an unconstitutional restriction on the dissemination of truthful commercial information. The use of a trade name, it explained, is a form of advertising because prospective customers may identify the name with a certain quality of service and goods. The district court rejected the equal protection attack on the board's membership, however, reasoning that the reservation of slots for members of the TOA was rationally related to faithful and vigilant enforcement of the Optometry Act.

Questions: (1) Does the First Amendment's protection of commercial speech condemn the Texas ban against the practice of optometry under a trade name? (2) Does the equal protection clause prohibit Texas from requiring a majority of the board entrusted with enforcement of the Optometry Act to belong to the TOA?

Decision: No to both questions. Opinion by Justice Powell. Vote: 7–2 on the first question and 9–0 on the second, Blackmun and Marshall dissenting in part.

Reasons: The decisions in *Bates* v. *State Bar of Arizona*, 433 U.S. 350 (1977) and *Virginia State Board of Pharmacy* v. *Virginia Citizens Consumer Council*, 425 U.S. 748 (1976) established two cardinal commercial speech principles. First, truthful commercial advertising may enjoy heightened constitutional solicitude if it relates to a basic service or necessity, conveys information of general public interest, and furthers the efficient allocation of resources by promoting informed consumer choices. Second, the First Amendment tolerates substantial regulation of commercial speech in order to forestall deceptive practices. This is because such speech is generally more verifiable than other utterances and more resistant to "chilling effects" because it is commercially inspired.

The use of trade names in the practice of optometry advances relatively unimportant First Amendment interests, whereas it offers numerous opportunities for deception. Trade names convey no information about an optometrist's prices and skills until they have acquired a public meaning over a period of time by recurrent association between the trade names and some standard of price or quality. On the other hand, trade names may be deceptively employed to attract customers when changes in the staff of optometrists have engendered concommitant changes in the quality of service. A trade name also allows disreputable optometrists to seek patronage by assuming different names. Finally, trade names facilitate mass advertising that can be employed to promote large-scale commercial practices with numerous branch offices. A state may legitimately discourage that type of professional or business growth.

The statutory ban on trade names also has solid roots in past abuses. It is justified, therefore, by the state interest in guarding the public from deception. It is significant, moreover, that little if any truthful commercial speech is suppressed by the ban. Factual information associated with trade names—price and quality of service—may be freely and explicitly communicated to the public.

Reserving a majority of the board's six seats to members of the TOA satisfies equal protection scrutiny if it is rationally founded. Competitive and regulatory struggles between commercial and professional optometrists in Texas preceded passage of the 1969 act, which largely incorporated the views of the latter. It was, therefore, reasonable for the legislature to entrust enforcement of the act to a board controlled by a professional organization that had demonstrated consistent support for its provisions. Due process, moreover, is not disturbed by the statutory failure to require a consumer representative on the board.

Voting and Elections

In a parade of cases headed by *Kramer* v. *Union Free School Dist.*, 395 U.S. 621 (1969),[1] the Court has invoked the equal protection clause of the Fourteenth Amendment to erase restrictions on the franchise.[2] Only a "compelling" government interest, the Court proclaimed in *Kramer*, can justify withholding the franchise from citizens sufficiently affected by the election being held.[3] Moreover, the Court declared, the disfranchisement must be "necessary" to promote the ascendent government interest.[4] This term, a 6–3 majority corralled the *Kramer* equal protection principles in *Holt Civic Club* v. *City of Tuscaloosa*, 439 U.S. 60 (1978). The compelling interest standard of equal protection review, the Court asserted, applies only when the contested disfranchisement is aimed at individuals residing within the geographic boundaries of the political unit conducting the election. Accordingly, the Court declared, an Alabama statute denying the municipal franchise to persons residing outside city limits but governed by the city's police jurisdiction could survive constitutional scrutiny with only a rational basis. Alabama, the Court speculated, might rationally have chosen to extend municipal police jurisdiction beyond city borders either as a prelude to annexation or as an efficient means of delivering municipal services. The equal protection clause, therefore, was not disturbed by Alabama's refusal to extend the municipal franchise to noncity residents.

The Court embraced a sweeping interpretation of the Voting Rights Act, which was designed to forestall racial discrimination. In *Dougherty County* v. *White*, 439 U.S. 32 (1978), Justice Marshall, writing for a 5–4 majority, declared that a county school board could not unilaterally require its employees to take unpaid leaves of absence to campaign for elective public office. The Voting Rights Act, Marshall

---

[1] Kramer invalidated a statute restricting eligibility to vote in schoolboard elections to persons who either had children enrolled in local schools or owned or leased property within the school district.
[2] Kramer was followed by Cipriano v. City of Houma, 395 U.S. 701 (1969) (invalidating a provision enfranchising only "property taxpayers" in an election to approve the issuance of revenue bonds by a municipal utility); Evans v. Cornman, 398 U.S. 419 (1970) (invalidating a state statute disfranchising persons residing on a federal enclave within the state); Phoenix v. Kolodziejski, 399 U.S. 204 (1970) (invalidating a restriction on the franchise in elections to approve the issuance of general obligation bonds to finance municipal improvements to real property taxpayers whose taxes would service the indebtedness); Hill v. Stone, 421 U.S. 289 (1975) (invalidating a restriction on the franchise in a local bond election to authorize construction of a library to persons paying real or personal property taxes).
[3] 395 U.S. at 627.
[4] Id.

asserted, required submission of the rule to either the U.S. attorney general or a federal district court to confirm an absence of any racially discriminatory purpose or effect before it could be ordained as law. Rules affecting electoral candidacy in states governed by the act, Marshall maintained, must undergo this preclearance if a potential for racial discrimination can be conceived.

In a third encounter with the political process, the Court unanimously invalidated an Illinois statute requiring political parties and independent candidates to gather more signatures to appear on Chicago election ballots than were necessary to appear on statewide ballots (*Illinois State Board of Elections* v. *Socialist Workers Party*, 440 U.S. 173 [1979]). The disparity, Justice Marshall stated, was repugnant to the equal protection clause because it needlessly burdened the twin rights of political association and of voting amalgamation regardless of political persuasion.

Holt Civic Club v. *City of Tuscaloosa*, 439 U.S. 60 (1978)

Facts: Alabama law requires municipalities to exercise police jurisdiction over unincorporated communities located within three miles of their city limits. Residents within these communities are governed by the municipality's criminal laws, police and sanitary regulations, and business licensing code, but are denied the franchise in city elections. License fees exacted from businesses in the communities, however, are only one-half the fees chargeable to businesses inside a city's limits. Residents of an unincorporated community brought suit claiming that they could not constitutionally be governed by a city's police jurisdiction unless they were offered the franchise on an equal footing with city residents. A three-judge federal district court rejected the claim, which was founded on the equal protection clause of the Fourteenth Amendment.

Question: Does Alabama's statute that requires the extraterritorial exercise of a city's police powers over nearby unincorporated communities violate the equal protection clause?

Decision: No. Opinion by Justice Rehnquist. Vote: 6–3, Brennan, White, and Marshall dissenting.

Reasons: The equal protection principle established by *Kramer* v. *Union Free School Dist.*, 395 U.S. 621 (1969), and its progeny is that municipalities may deny the franchise to its residents only when this can be justified by a compelling government interest. On the other hand, a second line of cases has uniformly recognized that a government may exclude from its political processes persons residing beyond its borders if that choice is rationally founded. The issue here is more akin to disfranchisement based on geographical boundaries than to the types of disfranchisement encountered in expounding the *Kramer* principle.

> [To agree] that extraterritorial extension of municipal powers requires concomitant extraterritorial extension of the franchise proves too much. . . . A city's decisions inescapably affect individuals living immediately outside its borders. The granting of building permits for highrise apartments, industrial plants, and the like on the city's fringe unavoidably contributes to problems of traffic congestion, school districting, and law enforcement immediately outside the city. . . . Yet no one would suggest that nonresidents likely to be affected by this sort of municipal action have a constitutional right to participate in the political processes bringing it about.

Alabama's decision to require municipalities to exercise police jurisdiction over adjacent unincorporated communities survives equal protection scrutiny because one can conceive of rational reasons for this distribution of government authority. Alabama may have thought this jurisdiction would be an appropriate prelude to annexation of unincorporated communities to the city proper. It may also have believed that basic municipal services such as police, fire, and health protection could be offered to such communities efficiently and cheaply by the extraterritorial application of a city's police jurisdiction. Residents of unincorporated communities, moreover, are shielded against extortionate revenue collection by the city government since their license fees are statutorily limited to half the amount exacted from city residents. In sum, Alabama's system of municipal police jurisdiction falls within "the extraordinary wide latitude that states have in creating various types of political subdivisions and conferring authority upon them."

Dougherty County, Georgia, Board of Education v. White, 439 U.S. 32 (1978)

Facts: Section 5 of the Voting Rights Act of 1965 requires all covered states and political subdivisions to obtain the approval of either the U.S. attorney general or a federal district court before imposing any new "standard, practice, or procedure with respect to voting. . . ." Approval will be granted only if it is determined that the proposal has neither a racially discriminatory purpose nor effect. A county school board in a state (Georgia) covered by the act adopted a rule requiring its employees to take unpaid leaves of absence during any period in which they were campaigning for elective public office. It did not, however, submit the rule for approval to either the attorney general or the federal district court. A black employee of the county who sought election to the Georgia General Assembly obtained an injunction against enforcement of the rule on the ground that it was subject to the preclearance requirements of the act.

Question: Was the county school board rule requiring leave for employee candidates seeking elective public office subject to the preclearance requirements of the Voting Rights Act?

Decision: Yes. Opinion by Justice Marshall. Vote: 5–4, Stewart, Powell, Burger, and Rehnquist dissenting.

Reasons: The phrase "standard, practice, or procedure with respect to voting" in section 5 should be expansively construed to embrace any enactment or proposal that would affect the eligibility of persons to become or remain candidates for public office. Otherwise, the overarching goal of the act—to eliminate and prevent any taint of racial discrimination in the electoral process—might be subverted.

In this case, the contested personnel rule discourages candidacy for public office by exacting a substantial economic sacrifice from employees seeking elective office. Moreover, its adoption came on the heels of the black plaintiff's announced candidacy for the General Assembly and without any past experience of high absenteeism among employees seeking office. Since the rule erected barriers to candidacy for public office in circumstances suggesting the potential for racial discrimination, it was a "standard, practice, or procedure with respect to voting."

The plaintiff contended, nevertheless, that preclearance was not required because the county school board is neither a state nor political subdivision within the meaning of the act. The teaching of *United States v. Board of Commissioners of Sheffield, Alabama*, 435 U.S. 110 (1978), however, is that any entity proposing a change affecting voting must submit it for preclearance review if it is located in a state covered by the act. Since the county school board was located in such a state, its contested rule was subject to preclearance whether or not it was also a political subdivision.

Illinois State Board of Elections v. *Socialist Workers Party,* 440 U.S. 173 (1979)

Facts: To appear on the ballot in statewide elections in Illinois, new political parties and independent candidates are required to gather supporting signatures of 25,000 qualified voters. In elections for offices of political subdivisions, however, ballot access can be obtained only if the supporting signatures amount to 5 percent of the number of persons who voted at the preceding election. As applied to the city of Chicago, this requirement excluded new parties or independent candidates from the ballot unless they obtained substantially more signatures than was required in statewide elections. A federal district court held that the discrepancy between the signature requirements for state and city elections violated the equal protection clause of the Fourteenth Amendment. The court of appeals affirmed.

Question: Do the Illinois signature requirements for new parties and independent candidates as applied in the city of Chicago violate the equal protection clause?

Decision: Yes. Opinion by Justice Marshall. Vote: 9–0.

Reasons: Restrictions on ballot access impinge upon two fundamental rights: the right to associate for political purposes and the right to cast one's vote effectively regardless of political persuasion. Curtailing these rights can be justified only by a compelling state interest. To forestall voter confusion and runoff elections, a state may legitimately reserve the ballot to serious candidates who have garnered a significant share of public support. But the equal protection clause demands that the state embrace "the least restrictive means" of achieving these objectives. Since Illinois has determined that overloading ballots in statewide elections can be avoided by a 25,000 supporting signature requirement, there is no rational reason to believe that a greater number of signatures is necessary to limit the size of ballots in Chicago.

Government Immunity

Claims of government immunity generally evoked an unsympathetic reception during the 1978–1979 term. The Court insisted on confining[1]

---

[1] In Gravel v. United States, 408 U.S. 606 (1972), the Court held that an arrangement for the private republication of the "Pentagon Papers" after a senator had placed them

the speech or debate clause protection bestowed on members of Congress to acts integral to the deliberative and communicative processes within the legislative branch in discharging its constitutional responsibilities. Neither the executive nor the judicial branches are permitted to use evidence of such legislative acts against a member. But press releases and newsletters intended to inform the public and other members, Chief Justice Burger declared for an 8–1 majority in *Hutchinson* v. *Proxmire*, 443 U.S. 111 (1979) (summary in section titled Freedom of Speech and Press), are too remote from the legislative process to shield the member from challenge by the executive or judicial branches. Accordingly, the Court held that alleged defamatory statements contained in press releases and newsletters issued by Senator Proxmire to publicize his "Golden Fleece" award lacked any speech or debate clause immunity. A 5–3 majority, however, resisted an attempt to curtail the scope of evidentiary immunity enjoyed by concededly legislative acts. In *United States* v. *Helstoski*, 442 U.S. 477 (1979), the Court rejected the prosecution's contention that using evidence of a legislative act to prove a congressman's motive for receiving money would not invade the protective ambit of the speech or debate clause. The *Helstoski* decision also erected formidable standards for demonstrating a waiver of speech or debate clause immunity, even assuming a waiver would be constitutionally cognizable.

The Eleventh Amendment generally insulates states from private suits in federal courts seeking retroactive liability payable from the state treasury. But in *Quern* v. *Jordan*, 440 U.S. 332 (1979), a unanimous Court held that the amendment could not restrain a federal court from ordering a state to apprise welfare recipients that an administrative forum would entertain claims of entitlement to past benefits that had been wrongfully withheld. The Court also unanimously refused in *Lake Country Estates, Inc.* v. *Tahoe Regional Planning Agency*, 440 U.S. 391 (1979), to invest the bi-state Tahoe Regional Planning Agency, funded by counties and controlled by designees of political subdivisions, with the Eleventh Amendment immunity conferred on states. The Court divided 5–3 in *Tahoe Regional Planning Agency*, however, in holding that the regional appointees of the agency enjoyed absolute immunity from damages for actions of a legislative character.

In *Nevada* v. *Hall* the state of Nevada was rebuffed in its quest to limit its liability in California state courts for wrongful acts that

---

in the public record during a subcommittee session was not a legislative act protected by the speech or debate clause. The Court stated that the contested republication was not essential to the deliberative or communicative process of Congress and that its investigation by the executive branch did not threaten legislative independence.

victimized California motorists. A Nevada statute imposes a $25,000 ceiling on recoverable damages in tort suits against the state. The full faith and credit clause of the U.S. Constitution and other provisions sympathetic to interstate comity, Nevada contended, required California courts to enforce the $25,000 ceiling in suits brought by motorists injured on California highways because of Nevada's misfeasance. Justice Stevens, speaking for a 6–3 majority, held that California could ignore the ceiling in order to preserve its general policy of complete redress for motor vehicle injuries.

United States v. Helstoski, 442 U.S. 477 (1979)

Facts: A congressman appeared before several grand juries investigating allegations that he had unlawfully received money from aliens for introducing private bills that would suspend the application of the immigration laws so as to permit them to remain in the country. In responding to questions and requests for documents, the congressman did not expressly base any recalcitrance on the speech or debate clause of the Constitution, Article I, Section 6, clause 1. Charged in a multi-count indictment with official corruption under 18 U.S. Code 201, the congressman moved to dismiss on the ground that the indictment violated the speech or debate clause. Refusing to dismiss, the district court nevertheless held that the clause prohibited the introduction of evidence of the performance of a legislative act during the government's case-in-chief. The court of appeals affirmed.

Question: Does the speech or debate clause prevent the use of evidence of past legislative acts in the government's case-in-chief against the congressman?

Decision: Yes. Opinion by Chief Justice Burger. Vote: 5–3, Stevens, Stewart, and Brennan dissenting, Powell not participating.

Reasons: The speech or debate clause, as expounded in *United States v. Johnson*, 383 U.S.169 (1966), and *United States v. Brewster*, 408 U.S. 501 (1972), unequivocally proscribes the use of evidence from a congressman's previous legislative acts to substantiate charges under 18 U.S. Code 201. The proscription, however, does not taint evidence of a promise to perform a legislative act. Discussions and correspondence originating outside the legislative process but which refer to legislative acts, the government contends, also fall outside the protection of the speech or debate clause if used to prove the congressman's motive for taking money but not the inspiration for his legislative acts. The clause, however, is absolute in shielding congressmen from the use of evidence of legislative acts for any purpose in a criminal prosecution under section 201.

The government claims that the congressman waived his speech or debate clause protection by cooperating with several grand juries. Since the clause incorporates an institutional mainstay against intimidation of members of Congress by the executive or the judiciary, whether its protection can be waived by an individual member is problematic. But assuming an affirmative answer, "waiver can be found only after explicit and unequivocal renunciation of the protection." No such evidence demonstrated waiver by the congressman in this case. The government alternatively argues that the enactment of section 201 constituted an institutional waiver of the clause by Congress. Even assuming that Congress may discard the protections of the clause through legislation, explicit and unequivocal expression would be required to accomplish the waiver. The language and legislative history of section 201 fail to evince a congressional intent to strip its members of speech or debate clause protection.

Quern v. Jordan, 440 U.S. 332 (1979)

Facts: In *Edelman* v. *Jordan*, 415 U.S. 651 (1974), the Court held that the Eleventh Amendment proscribes federal courts in private suits against states from compelling the retroactive payment of welfare benefits that had been wrongfully denied. Thereafter, a federal court of appeals concluded that neither *Edelman* nor the Eleventh Amendment precluded a remedial order requiring the state of Illinois to inform welfare recipients, in a regular monthly mailing, that a state administrative procedure was available to determine whether they were entitled to past welfare benefits.

Question: Is the Eleventh Amendment violated by a federal court order in a private suit that compels a state to advise welfare recipients that an administrative forum is available to determine their entitlement to past benefits that were wrongfully denied?

Decision: No. Opinion by Justice Rehnquist. Vote: 9–0.

Reasons: The Eleventh Amendment prohibits federal court orders in private suits that impose a retroactive liability that must be paid from public funds in the state treasury. Prospective relief, in contrast, escapes Eleventh Amendment reproach whether or not compliance will necessitate the expenditure of some state funds. In this case, the notice sanctioned by the court of appeals simply apprises welfare recipients of a state forum where claims to retroactive benefits may be determined. The notice neither requires that retroactive benefits be pursued nor awarded. And no objection was raised by the state to the expense of preparing and mailing the notice. The contested notice is more akin to prospective relief outside the ambit of the Eleventh Amendment than to retroactive relief that will be satisfied from state coffers.

The contention that Congress intended to curtail Eleventh Amendment immunity through the enactment of the Civil Rights Act of 1871, 42 U.S. Code 1983, however, is untenable and cannot justify remedial relief otherwise barred by the amendment.

Lake Country Estates, Inc. v. *Tahoe Regional Planning Agency,* 440 U.S. 391 (1979)

Facts: To coordinate and regulate development of the Lake Tahoe Basin and to conserve its natural resources, California and Nevada, with the consent of Congress, made a compact that created the Tahoe Regional Planning Agency. The TRPA is empowered to adopt and to enforce a regional plan for land use, transportation, conservation, recreation, and public services. Property owners in the Lake Tahoe Basin sued the TRPA and its individual members for damages in federal district court. They alleged that the adoption of a land use ordinance by the defendants that lowered the economic value of their property constituted a taking without just compensation as required by the Fifth and Fourteenth Amendments. The district court dismissed the complaint, but the court of appeals reversed in part. It sustained the dismissal as to the TRPA, reasoning that it was protected from suit in federal court by the Eleventh Amendment. With respect to the individual members of the TRPA, the court of appeals held that conduct of a legislative character was clothed with absolute immunity, whereas executive action was entitled to only a qualified immunity. Because the record failed to disclose whether the conduct at issue was legislative or executive, the court of appeals remanded for a hearing.

Questions: (1) Does the TRPA enjoy the immunity from suit in federal courts offered to states by the Eleventh Amendment? (2) Do the individual members of the TRPA enjoy absolute immunity from damages when acting in a legislative capacity?

Decision: No to the first question and yes to the second. Opinion by Justice Stevens. Vote: 9–0 on the first question and 6–3 on the second, Brennan, Marshall, and Blackmun dissenting in part.

Reasons: The express terms of the Eleventh Amendment restrict its immunity shield to states. Past decisions have refused to include political subdivisions such as counties and municipalities within the amendment's ambit, even though they exercise a portion of state power.

> If an interstate compact discloses that the compacting States created an agency comparable to a county or municipality . . . the Amendment should not be construed to immunize such an entity.

The compact creating the TRPA reveals an unequivocal intent that it be treated as a political subdivision rather than as an arm of the states. The TRPA is funded by counties in California and Nevada; a majority of its ten members are appointed by counties and cities; and judgments against TRPA are not binding on either Nevada or California. In addition, the TRPA's regulation of land use is traditionally a local government function and is not subject to veto at the state level. Accordingly, there is no good reason for conferring Eleventh Amendment immunity on the TRPA.

The appointed members of the TRPA, however, are entitled to absolute immunity from damages for actions of a legislative character. State and federal legislators have traditionally enjoyed such immunity under common law, federal statutes, and federal and state constitutions. The purpose of the immunity is to spare legislators from the harassment, distractions, and chilling effects on the uninhibited discharge of their duties that would be threatened by exposure to damage suits. Regional legislators need the same immunity from suit to encourage the fearless discharge of their legislative duties that is beneficial to the public good. Simply because TRPA members are appointed rather than elected and are not subject to discipline for misconduct by a legislative body does not alter this conclusion.

Nevada v. *Hall,* 440 U.S. 410 (1979)

Facts: California residents were injured in an automobile collision with a vehicle driven by an employee of the University of Nevada, an institution owned by the state. The accident occurred in California but during the employee's conduct of official business for Nevada. A negligence suit was brought against the state of Nevada in a California state court. Nevada moved to limit recoverable damages to $25,000 as provided by a Nevada statute governing torts suits against the state. The full faith and credit clause of the U.S. Constitution, Article IV, Section 1, it was claimed, required California courts to enforce the Nevada statute. The motion was denied, damages in excess of $1 million were awarded against Nevada, and a state appellate court affirmed the judgment.

Question: Did either the full faith and credit clause or any other constitutional provision require California courts to enforce Nevada's statute limiting the liability of the state in tort actions?

Decision: No. Opinion by Justice Stevens. Vote: 6–3, Burger, Rehnquist, and Blackmun dissenting.

Reasons: The full faith and credit clause requires each state to respect the official acts of other states. When jurisdiction has been properly asserted, a judgment in one state must be recognized in other states. In limited situations, moreover, the court of one state must apply statutory law of another state. The teaching of *Pacific Insurance Company* v. *Industrial Accident Commission*, 306 U.S. 493 (1939), however, is that a state may decline to enforce another state's law in order to preserve its own legitimate public policy.

In this case, California state courts refused to apply Nevada's restrictive liability statute to protect California's interest in offering full protection to persons injured on its highways through the negligence of either residents or nonresidents. To advance this interest, California has waived its own immunity from liability for wrongful acts committed by its agents and has authorized full recovery. Since application of a $25,000 recovery ceiling as provided in the Nevada statute would frustrate California's full recovery policy, it is not demanded by the full faith and credit clause.

Other constitutional provisions, such as the privileges and immunities protections offered to state citizens in Article IV, Section 2, circumscribe state sovereignty to promote comity among states. But none commands a state to enforce the statutes of other states against its will, at least when the refusal is necessary to uphold its equally legitimate laws.

It may be wise policy, as a matter of harmonious interstate relations, for States to accord each other immunity or to respect any established limits of liability. . . . But if a federal court were to hold, by inference from the structure of our Constitution and nothing else, that California is not free in this case to enforce its policy of full compensation, that holding would constitute the real intrusion on sovereignty of the States—and the power of the people—in our Union.

Civil Rights and Civil Liberties

A recurrent theme in the Court's major encounters with asserted claims of civil rights or civil liberties was deference to official authority and legislative choices. Major attention was devoted to expounding the mandates of procedural due process.

In *Parham* v. *J.R.*, 442 U.S. 584 (1979), a 6–3 majority ruled that a minor lacks any due process right to an adversary hearing prior to commitment in a state mental health care hospital at the request of parents, guardians, or state custodians. Writing for the Court, Chief Justice Burger declared that the law may legitimately presume that parents will act to further the best interests of their children.[1] Nevertheless, Burger stated, procedural due process requires substantial safeguards to protect a child against wrongful commitment: the final commitment decision must be made by an independent and neutral factfinder; the decision must be founded on a painstaking inquiry into the child's mental and emotional condition by employing traditional medical investigative techniques; and the child's continuing need for commitment must be reviewed periodically, pursuant to procedures comparable to those obligatory in making the initial commitment decision.

Procedural due process precepts governing decisions on whether to grant or deny discretionary parole were contested in *Greenholtz* v. *Nebraska Penal and Correctional Complex Inmates*, 442 U.S. 1 (1979). Due process, the Court ruled, did not entitle inmates to either a full formal hearing or to an enumeration of the factors relevant to the parole decision. The Court declared, moreover, that parole could be denied without setting out the evidentiary foundation for the decision. Communicating the reasons for the denial was constitutionally sufficient.

Emphasizing the paramount interest in highway safety, a 5–4 majority in *Mackey* v. *Montrym*, 443 U.S. 1 (1979), detected no due process flaw in a summary ninety-day suspension of a driver's license because an arrestee refused to submit to a breathalyzer test. Writing

---

[1] In contrast, the ruling in Bellotti v. Baird, 443 U.S. 622 (1979), disclaimed any natural congruence of interests between parents and minors in making an abortion decision.

for the Court, Chief Justice Burger pointed out that upon surrendering his license, the arrestee could demand an immediate hearing to challenge the validity of the suspension.

The suspension of a horse training license provoked the procedural due process dispute in *Barry* v. *Barchi*, 443 U.S. 55 (1979). There the Court ruled that a trainer's license could be summarily suspended for fifteen days if there was probable cause to believe that the drugging of a horse he had trained could be ascribed to his negligence. But, the Court added, due process guaranteed the aggrieved trainer a prompt post-suspension hearing to resolve controverted issues.

Procedural due process complaints asserted in *Califano* v. *Yamasaki*, 442 U.S. 682 (1979), and *Leis* v. *Flynt*, 439 U.S. 438 (1979), failed to elicit the Court's sympathy. In the former, the Court found no due process infirmity in denying an oral hearing before recoupment commenced of alleged overpayments made to social security beneficiaries. In the latter, a 5–4 majority concluded that procedural due process affords no protection to an out-of-state attorney's interest in special appearances before courts entrusted with discretion over the matter.

Adults resisting commitment to a mental hospital for an indefinite period achieved a modest due process victory in *Addington* v. *Texas*, 441 U.S. 418 (1979). By a vote of 8–0, the Court ruled that due process demanded that the requisite findings justifying commitment—mental illness and a need for self-protection or the protection of others—be made on the basis of clear and convincing evidence.

The Court focused on equal protection precepts in *Lalli* v. *Lalli*, 439 U.S. 259 (1978), and *Califano* v. *Boles*, 443 U.S. 282 (1979).

In *Lalli*, a 5–4 majority sustained a statute that denied illegitimate children rights to their fathers' estates unless a judicial order of filiation declaring paternity had been made during the father's life. Writing for a plurality, Justice Powell declared that the strong state interest in the swift and orderly disposition of property at death justified the statutory discrimination against illegitimates. A majority agreed in *Lalli*, however, that classifications founded on illegitimacy must be "substantially related to permissible state interests" to survive equal protection review.

In *Califano* v. *Boles*, the Court rejected the view that to deny social security insurance benefits to mothers of illegitimate children was tantamount to discrimination against illegitimates. Speaking for a five-member majority, Justice Rehnquist asserted that a statutory classification inferred from its disparate impact is cognizable under the equal protection clause only upon a showing "that the class that

is purportedly discriminated against . . . suffers significant deprivation of a benefit or imposition of a substantial burden."

The Court maintained its recent display of antipathy toward
encumbering the operations of jail and prison facilities with constitutional safeguards.[2] In *Bell* v. *Wolfish*, 441 U.S. 520 (1979), a majority
sustained the constitutionality of institutional rules that prohibited
pretrial detainees from receiving hardcover books, unless directly
mailed by publishers, book clubs, or bookstores, and from receiving
packages containing food or personal property. The Court further
held that the detainees lacked any Fourth Amendment protection
against body cavity inspections following contacts with visitors or
against exclusion from their rooms during routine unannounced
searches. Due process, the Court also declared, does not proscribe
double-bunking of detainees. Exhibiting reflexive deference to fears
for institutional order and security voiced by correctional officials, the
Court inveighed against judicial intervention into prison management
in the guise of constitutional considerations.

A schism in a local Presbyterian church and an ensuing quarrel
over church property precipitated the litigation in *Jones* v. *Wolf*, 443
U.S. 595 (1979). There a 5–4 majority proclaimed that civil courts may
resolve church property disputes without disturbing the First Amendment's protection of religious freedom so long as "neutral principles
of law" are employed. Writing for the Court, Justice Blackmun maintained that application of neutral principles would permit religious
organizations to ensure that the disposition of church property accords with the desires of its members through reversionary clauses,

---

[2] See Jones v. North Carolina Prisoners Labor Union, 433 U.S. 119 (1977) (upholding
prison ban on union solicitation and meetings and refusal to deliver bulk mailings from
and concerning a union for redistribution among inmates); Meachum v. Fano, 427 U.S.
215 (1976) (denying inmates due process protection before transfer from a medium-
security prison institution); Baxter v. Palmingiano, 425 U.S. 308 (1976) (holding that
in prison disciplinary proceedings, an inmate lacks a right to counsel, to a statement
of reasons for denying an opportunity for cross-examination, and to prohibit adverse
inferences drawn from his failure to testify); Pell v. Procunier, 417 U.S. 817 (1974)
(holding that neither inmates nor journalists have a First Amendment right to arrange
interviews). The Court has also recognized an array of prison rights. See Hutto v.
Finney, 439 U.S. 1122 (1978) (right against cruel and unusual prison conditions); Bounds
v. Smith, 430 U.S. 817 (1977) (right to law library or comparable legal assistance); Estelle
v. Gamble, 429 U.S. 97 (1976) (right to minimum level of medical care); Procunier v.
Martinez, 416 U.S. 396 (1974) (right of access to the courts, right against overbroad
mail censorship regulations, and right to procedural safeguards in connection with a
validly drawn censorship scheme); Wolff v. McDonnell, 418 U.S. 539 (1974) (right to
due process safeguards before loss of good-time credits or confinement to a disciplinary
cell, right to legal assistance to prepare civil rights suit); O'Brien v. Skinner, 414 U.S.
524 (1974) (equal protection right prohibiting arbitrary discrimination in offering ab-
sentee ballots to inmates).

trust provisions, and the express designation of authority to determine ownership in the event of a schism.

A statutory burden on the constitutional right of foreign travel was examined in *Califano* v. *Aznavarian*, 439 U.S. 170 (1979). Without dissent, the Court held that temporary termination of social security benefits to recipients who leave the United States for an entire month does not saddle those who exercise the right of international travel with an impermissible burden.

The Court unanimously agreed on a pioneering exposition of the protection afforded handicapped persons by section 504 of the Rehabilitation Act. The act prohibits discrimination against an "otherwise qualified handicapped individual" in federally funded programs "solely by reasons of his handicap." But in *Southeastern Community College* v. *Davis*, 442 U.S. 397 (1979), the Court asserted that section 504 does not impose any affirmative action obligation to substantially modify or lower program standards in order to accommodate the limitations of a handicapped applicant. Rather, the Court declared, handicaps may legitimately be considered in determining whether an applicant is qualified for a federally funded program. Accordingly, it held that an applicant's serious hearing disability justified the denial of her admission into a state community college nursing program.

Parham v. *J. R.*, 442 U.S. 584 (1979)

Facts: A class-action suit filed in federal district court challenged the constitutionality of Georgia procedures that govern requests by parents, guardians, or state custodians to commit minor children to state-operated mental health care institutions. Georgia statutes empower the superintendents at various regional mental health hospitals to admit temporarily any child for observation and diagnosis at the behest of his parents, guardian, or state custodian. Commitment to the hospital is conditioned on findings of mental illness and suitability for treatment. Any child hospitalized for more than five days may be discharged at the request of a parent or guardian, and superintendents are obligated to release children who have either recovered or whose continued stay is contrary to their best interests. The archetypal procedures for admitting minors to the regional hospitals entrust the ultimate decision to a state physician. He considers staff interviews with the child and his parents or guardian, other outside sources of information about the child, and recommendations by hospital or community health center staff. After admittance, a child's condition and continuing need for hospital care is reviewed periodically, ordinarily at two-week intervals, by at least one independent medical review group. The district court held that the procedures were flawed under the due process clause of the Fourteenth Amendment in failing to guarantee children an adversary hearing before an impartial tribunal prior to commitment.

Question: Do Georgia's procedures for admitting children to state mental health care hospitals at the request of parents, guardians, or state custodians contravene constitutional due process?

Decision: No. Opinion by Chief Justice Burger. Vote: 6–3, Brennan, Marshall, and Stevens dissenting in part.

Reasons: The requirements of procedural due process are charted by three considerations: the private interests affected by the official action, the risk of erroneous deprivation of those interests through the procedures used, and the government interests at stake. The voluntary commitment procedures employed by Georgia's state mental health hospitals affect the private interests of both children and their parents. A child has a constitutionally recognized interest in avoiding unnecessary mental health care treatment that curtails physical freedom and may beget social stigma. Parents, on the other hand, are constitutionally invested with broad authority over minor children. In the absence of proof of neglect or abuse, the law ordinarily presumes that parental actions are congruent with the best interests of their children. This presumption accords with volumes of human experience. Although curtailment of parental authority over children to forestall physical or mental harm can be countenanced, the record in this case fails to document a single instance of bad faith by any parent seeking commitment of a child plaintiff. Moreover, the parental decision to seek commitment is subservient to the independent judgment of hospital superintendents as to the child's need for confinement. In sum, a state may permit parents, when there is no finding of abuse or neglect, to retain a substantial role in determining whether a child should be institutionalized for mental health care treatment. The child's rights and the nature of the commitment decision are such, however, that the parental choice cannot always be final and unreviewable.

Several state interests are safeguarded by employing the contested procedures. They reserve the use of costly mental health facilities to those in genuine need. The lack of precommitment adversary proceedings encourages parents to seek help for their children by reducing the likelihood of family discord and inquiry into embarrassing private matters. The omission of an adversary hearing also permits psychiatrists, psychologists, and other behavioral specialists to spend more time diagnosing and treating patients.

Procedural due process is also concerned with the risk of official error.

> We conclude that the risk of error inherent in the parental decision to have a child institutionalized for mental health care is sufficiently great that some kind of inquiry should be made by a neutral factfinder to determine whether the statutory requirements for admission are satisfied.

The inquiry must include an interview with the child and a full probe of his background by examining all available sources. A staff physician will suffice as the factfinder if he has final decision-making authority and evaluates independently the child's mental and emotional condition and need for treatment. The physician need not conduct a formal or quasi-formal hearing, but can rely on traditional medical investigative techniques. Due process does require, however, that the child's continuing need for commitment be reviewed periodically by independent procedures comparable to those obligatory in making the initial commitment decision.

Although these procedures are not an absolute safeguard against official error, the risk of error would not be appreciably reduced by employing formal, judicial type hearings. Procedural due process rules are animated by the risk of error inherent in the typical, not the exceptional, case.

The record in this case absolves Georgia's procedures for the voluntary commitment of children by parents or guardians from any constitutional infirmity. On remand, however, the district court should consider any individual claims of deviation from the general scheme in the initial commitment. It should also examine the constitutional adequacy of Georgia's procedures for determining whether a child's continuing confinement is necessary and appropriate. We have held only that periodic reviews are necessary to reduce the risk of error in the initial admission.

Finally, we hold that children who are wards of the state enjoy no greater procedural safeguards than children of natural parents regarding voluntary admissions to the state's mental health hospitals. By statute, the state is directed to act in the child's best interest, and the record discloses nothing casting doubt on fidelity to that command. Accordingly, the state agency with custody and control of the child in the place of parents may be given authority to play the same role as natural parents in the initial commitment process. It is possible, however, that the procedures required in reviewing a ward's need for continuing care should be different from those used to review a child with natural parents because the former lacks the protective scrutiny of a concerned family. This issue should be explored in the first instance on remand in the district court.

Greenholtz v. Inmates of the Nebraska Penal and Correctional Complex, 442 U.S. 1 (1979)

Facts: Inmates of a Nebraska penal institution challenged the constitutionality of procedures used by the board of parole to determine whether to grant or deny discretionary parole. At least once a year every inmate receives an initial parole review hearing consisting of the board's examination of the inmate's entire preconfinement and postconfinement record, an interview with the inmate, and any letters or statements the inmate offers to support a grant of parole. If the board denies parole after the initial review hearing, it informs the inmate of the reasons for its action. If the initial review hearing convinces the board that an inmate is a good candidate for release, a final hearing is scheduled. The inmate is notified of the month of the final hearing, and may present evidence, call witnesses, and be represented by counsel. If parole is denied, a written statement of the reasons for the denial is provided within thirty days.

The district court held that the discretionary parole procedures offended constitutional due process, and the court of appeals, with some modifications, affirmed. It declared, among other things, that procedural due process entitled every inmate eligible for parole to a full formal hearing, written notice, reasonably in advance of the hearing, including a list of factors relevant to the parole decision, and a statement of the evidence relied upon if parole is denied.

Question: Are the procedures used by the Nebraska board of parole in determining whether to grant discretionary parole constitutionally defective?

Decision: No. Opinion by Chief Justice Burger. Vote: 5–4, Powell, Marshall, Brennan, and Stevens dissenting in part.

Reasons: Procedural due process guarantees are applicable to constitutionally protected "liberty" interests. As expounded in *Board of Regents* v. *Roth,* 408 U.S. 564 (1972), these protectable liberty interests consist of legitimate claims of entitlement. Two theories are advanced to support the view that Nebraska inmates possess a protected liberty interest in a parole determination.

It is argued that where, as here, a state offers the possibility of parole, a protectable expectation of liberty is created. The rationale of *Morrissey* v. *Brewer*, 408 U.S. 471 (1972), it is claimed, confirms this conclusion. *Morrissey*, however, held only that a parole revocation hearing triggered due process safeguards. There is a palpable distinction between losing a liberty one has, as in a revoked parole, and having a hope of conditional freedom disappointed. A decision to terminate parole, moreover, entails a dual inquiry into whether a condition of parole has been violated and whether revocation is an appropriate sanction. The parole release decision, in contrast, is freighted with imponderables and involves large elements of prophecy. Accordingly, a state's offer of discretionary parole does not transform a "mere hope" that it will be granted into an interest protected by due process.

A Nebraska statute, the litigant nevertheless maintained, creates a protectable expectation of parole. It provides that parole shall be granted unless there is a finding by the board that any of four specifically enumerated reasons justifies denial. Given the statute's unique structure and language, some measure of due process protection should be extended to a Nebraska inmate's expectancy of release.

Flexibility is the hallmark of sound procedural due process. Minimizing the risk of error is its central focus. The board of parole is invested with wide discretion in making parole release decisions in partial acknowledgement that precise standards of guidance cannot be devised. The parole decision entails problematical analysis of psychological factors and predictions of future behavior. In addition, encumbering parole decisions with burdensome procedures may create an adversary relation between society and the inmate and frustrate rehabilitation objectives. Guided by these considerations, the contested parole procedures satisfy due process.

The court of appeals erred in prescribing a formal hearing for every inmate. At best, the requirement would negligibly decrease the risk of error. The initial review hearing offers the inmate a fair opportunity to present his case for parole through an interview and written statement and to ensure that the behavior records before the board relate to his case. "Since the [parole] decision is one that must be made largely on the basis of the inmate's files, this procedure adequately safeguards against serious risks of error and thus satisfies due process."

Requiring the board to specify the particular evidence underlying denials of parole was also constitutionally unwarranted. It would tend to convert the parole process into an adversary proceeding and would frequently be futile since the denials are often based on a host of imponderables. In sum, the board's practice of simply communicating the reasons for denying parole is irreproachable.

Finally, the notice rule mandated by the court of appeals lacks any constitutional base. At present, an inmate receives advance notice of the month of a formal hearing, and the exact time of the hearing is posted on the day it is held. In the absence of any claim that either the timing or substance of the notice seriously prejudices the inmate's preparation for the hearing, the notice is constitutionally unassailable.

Mackey v. Montrym, 443 U.S. 1 (1979)

Facts: A Massachusetts statute automatically suspends a driver's license for refusing to take a breathalyzer test after an arrest for drunk driving. It directs the police officer who witnesses the arrestee's refusal to prepare a written report under oath, endorsed by a third party witness to the event. The officer is also required to describe the foundation for his belief that the arrestee had been driving under the influence of intoxicating liquor and to obtain the police chief's endorsement of his report. Upon receipt of a report that complies with the statutory formalities, the Massachusetts registrar of motor vehicles is obligated to suspend the arrestee's license for ninety days. Upon surrendering his license, however, the arrestee may obtain an immediate hearing before the registrar to challenge the accuracy of the police report and the validity of the suspension. A three-judge federal district court held that the statutory omission of an opportunity for a presuspension hearing offended the procedural due process command of the Fourteenth Amendment.

Question: Do the Massachusetts statutory provisions for suspending a driver's license after an arrestee's refusal to take a breathalyzer test violate procedural due process?

Decision: No. Opinion by Chief Justice Burger. Vote: 5–4, Stewart, Brennan, Marshall, and Stevens dissenting.

Reasons: A driver's license is a form of property, the Court held in *Bell* v. *Burson*, 402 U.S. 535 (1971), that may not be revoked or suspended unless procedural due process safeguards are followed. The content of these safeguards, the Court ruled in *Mathews* v. *Eldridge*, 424 U.S. 319 (1976), turns on three factors: the importance

113

of the private interest affected by the official action, the risk of erroneous action created by the procedures used and the ability to reduce that risk by substitute or additional procedures, and the government interest at stake, including the fiscal and administrative burdens that the proffered alternative procedures would entail.

An individual has a substantial interest in the continuous possession and use of a driver's license until a hearing is offered to contest any attempted suspension. The Massachusetts statute, however, poses only a modest threat to this interest by limiting any suspension to ninety days and offering a hearing immediately after suspension commences.

The statutory procedures also offer reasonable safeguards against erroneous suspension by the registrar of motor vehicles. The predicates for suspension—a drunk driving arrest based on probable cause coupled with a refusal to take a breathalyzer test—are objective facts either within the personal knowledge of an impartial government official or readily ascertainable by him. The arresting officer is subject to civil liability for an unlawful arrest and to criminal penalties for deliberately misrepresenting facts. The refusal to submit to a breathalyzer test must be witnessed by two officers, and the police report that triggers suspension must be endorsed by the police chief. Finally, the registrar will ordinarily detect any clerical errors or other deficiencies in the report that would taint a suspension.

A presuspension hearing would not substantially strengthen the existing procedural safeguards. It would offer only a bootless opportunity to resolve factual disputes concerning the police report because the registrar lacks discretion to stay any license suspension if the report complies with the requisite statutory formalities. Since the legislative judgment to deny the registrar discretion was not irrational, the value of a presuspension hearing cannot be tested by presuming the existence of discretion.

The government interest in highway safety is paramount. The summary suspension procedures for a driver's refusal to take a breathalyzer test upon arrest for drunk driving provide a threefold protection of this interest: drunk driving is deterred, drunk drivers are promptly removed from the public highways, and arrestees are induced to take breathalyzer tests and thereby create reliable evidence for use in subsequent criminal proceedings. A presuspension hearing, moreover, would jeopardize public safety by encouraging resistance to the breathalyzer test and the misuse of the hearing for delaying purposes. Finally, the incentive to delay offered by a presuspension hearing would escalate the number of such hearings and subject the state to substantial fiscal and administrative burdens.

We therefore conclude that procedural due process precepts are not disturbed by the statutory procedures for summarily suspending a driver's license coupled with an immediate opportunity for a post-suspension hearing.

Barry v. Barchi, 443 U.S. 55 (1979)

Facts: The New York State Racing and Wagering Board is empowered to license horse trainers participating in harness horse racing and to establish standards of conduct for retaining licenses. The board forbids the drugging of horses within forty-eight hours of a race and holds trainers accountable for the condition of their horses before, during, and after a race. A trainer is prohibited from racing a horse that he knows or should have known has been drugged and is obligated to take reasonable measures to forestall drugging by any person unconnected with the horse owner or trainer. If a postrace test discloses the presence of drugs, it is rebuttably presumed that the drug was either administered by the trainer or the condition came about because of his negligence.

Relying on this evidentiary presumption, the state suspended a trainer's license for fifteen days after a postrace urinalysis revealed a stimulant drug in a horse he had trained. Forgoing his right to a postsuspension hearing before the board, the trainer assailed the constitutionality of the license suspension procedures in federal district court. Suspending the license of a harness race horse trainer, the court decided, inflicts irreparable injury. Accordingly, it held, the board's procedures were flawed under the due process clause for failing to guarantee allegedly culpable trainers either a presuspension or prompt postsuspension hearing. The court further concluded that the fewer procedural safeguards offered to trainers involved in harness racing in contrast to those engaged in thoroughbred racing lacked the rationality demanded by the equal protection clause of the Fourteenth Amendment.

Questions: (1) Do the board's procedures for summary suspensions of licenses held by trainers involved in harness racing violate due process? (2) Did the board's failure to guarantee the trainer in this case a prompt postsuspension hearing violate due process? (3) Does the equal protection clause proscribe the employment of greater procedural protections for trainers involved in thoroughbred racing than for their harness racing counterparts?

Decision: No to question 1, yes to question 2, and no to question 3. Opinion by Justice White. Vote: 5–0 on question 1, 9–0 on question 2, 5–0 on question 3, Brennan, Stewart, Marshall, and Stevens concurring in part.

Reasons: The board may suspend a trainer's license only upon proof that his horse had been drugged and that he was culpable. The concept of due process, however, is sufficiently flexible to tolerate interim license suspensions founded on probable cause pending a prompt judicial or administrative hearing that would definitely determine the culpability issue. Once probable cause is established, the state's interests in protecting the integrity of racing conducted under its auspices and in protecting the public from harm becomes acute, whereas the trainer's interest in avoiding baseless attacks on his professional reputation is reduced.

The presuspension procedures in this case established the probable cause necessary for a summary interim license suspension. An expert testified as to the tests and results that supported the charge that the trainer's horse had been drugged. The legal duties placed on the trainer, moreover, supported the statutory inference that the drugging was caused by him. And nothing the state investigators unearthed during their investigation provided convincing proof that he was not negligent.

Due process was violated, however, by the failure to guarantee the trainer a prompt postsuspension hearing to resolve disputed issues. All the law required was that the board offer a hearing at some unstated time and issue a decision thirty days thereafter. Weighing the severe consequences of a license suspension against the minimal state interest in deferring a hearing, we conclude that due process required a postsuspension hearing "without appreciable delay."

The equal protection issue emerges from the absence of any board authority to stay a license suspension for harness horse trainers pending a hearing. Such discretionary power is conferred with respect to trainers of thoroughbred horses. Legislative history, however, discloses that harness racing was afflicted with a degree of fraud and corruption not associated with thoroughbred racing and which explained more exacting regulation of the former. The mandatory interim suspension procedure applicable in the harness racing context was rationally related to the legislative goal of forestalling fraud and maintaining public confidence in the sport. No greater justification is required by the equal protection clause.

Califano v. *Yamasaki,* 442 U.S. 682 (1979)

Facts: Section 204(a)(1) of the Social Security Act empowers the secretary of the Department of Health, Education and Welfare to recover overpayments made to beneficiaries of the old-age, survivors', or disability programs by decreasing future payments. The secretary exercises this authority, in part, by making unilateral determinations that beneficiaries have been overpaid, and placing the burden on them to seek reconsideration of the accuracy of the findings. If reconsideration is requested in writing, recoupment is deferred pending a decision by a regional field office. If the decision is adverse to the recipient, monthly payments are reduced until the overpayment is recouped. The recipient, however, may appeal the regional office decision and recover amounts wrongfully recouped if he ultimately prevails. A federal district court held that the recoupment procedures violated procedural due process by failing to offer recipients a hearing to challenge overpayment findings prior to the reduction of monthly benefits. The court of appeals affirmed in part and reversed in part. When reconsideration was requested on the ground that computational or payment errors had been made, the court stated, a prior oral hearing was not necessary, since the dispute could be resolved without evaluating credibility. But if credibility issues were raised by the reconsideration request, the court declared, procedural due process commanded an oral hearing before recoupment could commence.

Question: Do the secretary's procedures for recouping overpayments under section 204(a)(1) of the act violate procedural due process?

Decision: No. Opinion by Justice Blackmun. Vote: 8–0, Powell not participating.

Reasons: Requests for reconsideration under section 204(a)(1) raise relatively straightforward matters of computation. Written review will ordinarily be adequate to rectify prior mistakes. Simply because an exceptional case may raise credibility issues does not alter due process standards. The nature of a due process hearing is shaped by the risk of error in the truthfinding process in the generality of cases, not the unusual ones. Accordingly, we hold that due process is not disturbed by the secretary's failure to provide oral hearings prior to commencing recoupment under section 204(a)(1).

Leis v. Flynt, 439 U.S. 438 (1979)

Facts: An Ohio state judge summarily denied the request of out-of-state attorneys, not admitted to practice in Ohio, to appear specially *(pro hac vice)* to represent a criminal defendant. The attorneys obtained a federal district court injunction against further prosecution of the defendant until the state trial judge held a hearing on their *pro hac vice* applications. An attorney's interest in representing a client, the district court held, is a constitutionally protected right that may not be infringed without a hearing. The court of appeals affirmed.

Question: Did the out-of-state attorneys enjoy a constitutionally protected property right to *pro hac vice* appearances in representing clients before Ohio state courts?

Decision: No. *Per curiam* opinion. Vote: 5–4, Stevens, Brennan, and Marshall dissenting, White voting to set the case for oral argument.

Reasons: Property rights protected from infringement under the due process clause of the Fourteenth Amendment stem from independent sources outside the Constitution such as state or federal laws. No Ohio law entitles an out-of-state lawyer to appear *pro hac vice.* The approval of a *pro hac vice* appearance is entirely within the discretion of state trial judges. Neither does federal law create a property interest in *pro hac vice* appearances. Several decisions have affirmed the power of states to exclude out-of-state counsel altogether or on a case-by-case basis.

> Accordingly, because [the out-of-state attorneys] did not possess a cognizable property interest within the terms of the Fourteenth Amendment, the Constitution does not obligate the Ohio courts to accord them procedural due process in passing on their application for permission to appear pro hac vice. . . .

Addington v. Texas, 441 U.S. 418 (1979)

Facts: A Texas statute authorizes the involuntary commitment of an individual to a mental hospital for an indefinite period if two findings are made in a judicial proceeding: that the individual is mentally ill and that hospitalization is required for his own welfare or the protection of others. Addington was committed under the statute after a jury concluded that the requisite findings had been proved by "clear, unequivocal and convincing evidence." A state appellate court overturned the commitment, reasoning that constitutional due process required that the findings be proved beyond a reasonable doubt. But Addington's commitment order was reinstated by the Texas Supreme Court. It declared that due process permitted involuntary commitment if mental illness and a need for protection were proved by only a preponderance of the evidence.

Question: Does constitutional due process prohibit the involuntary and indefinite commitment of an individual to a mental hospital unless the requisite findings are proved by clear and convincing evidence?

Decision: Yes. Opinion by Chief Justice Burger. Vote: 8–0, Powell did not participate.

Reasons: Due process limits the choice of standards of proof for factfinding in adjudicatory proceedings. Its restrictions are marked by the "degree of confidence our society thinks [the factfinder] should have in the correctness of factual conclusions for a particular type of adjudication." Both the interests of society and the litigants must be weighed in determining constitutionally permissible standards of proof.

Where individual liberty is at stake, society and due process are loath to risk errors of fact finding that disadvantage the individual. In criminal cases, for instance, due process demands proof of guilt beyond a reasonable doubt. Civil commitment proceedings, like criminal cases, threaten loss of liberty and social stigma. The state, on the other hand, has a legitimate interest in caring for mentally ill citizens who pose some danger to themselves or to others. But the state has no interest in confining individuals who are not so afflicted. Use of a preponderance of the evidence standard in civil commitment proceedings increases the risk that individuals will be erroneously confined without advancing any state interest.

> At one time or another every person exhibits some abnormal behavior which might be perceived by some as symptomatic of a mental or emotional disorder, but which in fact is within a range of conduct that is generally acceptable . . . [T]here is the possible risk that a factfinder might decide to commit an individual based solely on a few isolated instances of unusual conduct. Increasing the burden of proof is one way

to impress the factfinder with the importance of the decision and thereby perhaps to reduce the chances that inappropriate commitments will be ordered.

In sum, due process prohibits a preponderance-of-the-evidence standard in civil commitment proceedings because it may beget errors of fact finding injurious to individual liberty without advancing any compensatory societal interest.

A reasonable doubt standard, on the other hand, is not constitutionally required. Unlike criminal cases, civil commitment proceedings are not inspired by punitive motives. An erroneous confinement, morever, may be corrected at recurrent intervals through the help of concerned relatives or by layers of professional review. In addition, those who are in fact mentally ill may be disadvantaged by erroneous decisions against confinement. Finally, the expert psychiatric testimony ordinarily encountered in commitment proceedings is so equivocal and impressionistic that it is doubtful whether a state could ever prove beyond a reasonable doubt that an individual is both mentally ill and likely to be dangerous.

An intermediate level of burden of proof between the preponderance and reasonable doubt standards fairly balances individual and state interests in civil commitment proceedings and marks the command of due process. It requires proof of facts by "clear and convincing" evidence but not by the more exacting standard of "clear, unequivocal and convincing" evidence employed by the jury in this case. Since the latter standard exceeds the constitutional minimum, the jury's findings that triggered Addington's commitment are beyond due process reproach.

Lalli v. Lalli, 439 U.S. 259 (1978)

Facts: A New York statute permits illegitimate children to inherit from their fathers by intestate succession only if, during the lifetime of the father, a judicial order declaring paternity has been made. No comparable inheritancy requirement restricts the rights of legitimate children. An illegitimate child denied inheritance rights, despite the fact that his deceased father openly and frequently acknowledged him as his son, sought to invalidate the statute under the equal protection clause of the Fourteenth Amendment. Concluding that the statute was invulnerable to equal protection reproach, the New York Court of Appeals maintained that it was reasonably tailored to further the state's interest in the orderly settlement of estates and the dependability of titles to property passing under intestacy laws.

Question: Is the contested inheritance statute flawed under the equal protection clause insofar as it discriminates against illegitimate children?

Decision: No. Plurality opinion by Justice Powell. Vote: 5–4, Blackmun and Rehnquist concurring, Brennan, White, Marshall, and Stevens dissenting.

Reasons: The decision in *Trimble* v. *Gordon,* 430 U.S. 762 (1977), contains several fundamental teachings regarding equal protection claims advanced by illegitimates. First, classifications on the basis of illegitimacy must be substantially related to permissible state interests. Second, illegitimates cannot be saddled with disadvantages for the purpose of discouraging illicit relationships. Third, the difficulties of proving paternity and the related danger of spurious claims against intestate estates may justify demanding a more exacting standard for illegitimate than legitimate children asserting rights to estates of their fathers.

The challenged statute in this case seeks to safeguard the important state interest in the orderly disposition of property at death. Paternity is difficult to prove for offspring of illicit relationships. The father may be ignorant of his child's birth or unconcerned with his future. The mother may also not know the identity of the father. If illegitimates were offered unrestricted rights of intestacy, compliance with procedural due process requirements in distributing their fathers' estates would be problematic since the identity of illegitimates would frequently be unknown. Even where identity is not a problem, the state has a legitimate interest in avoiding the difficulties of proving paternity and protecting reputations against unjust accusations in paternity proceedings. These multiple interests are substantially advanced by requiring judicial resolution of paternity disputes during the father's lifetime. It promotes accurate resolution of such disputes and facilitates the swift administration of intestate estates. The questioned statute, therefore, carries no equal protection taint, although it may unfairly deny inheritance rights to some illegitimates who could prove paternity without threatening disruption of the administration of estates. Statutory classifications cannot be placed under an equal protection cloud, however, just because they sometimes beget inequitable results.

Califano v. *Boles*, 443 U.S. 282 (1979)

Facts: The Social Security Act, 42 U.S. Code 402(g)(1), denies mother's insurance benefits to mothers not married to covered wage earners who fathered their illegitimate children. A federal district court invalidated the statute on the ground that it invidiously discriminated against illegitimate children in contravention of equal protection precepts. The chief statutory purpose of section 402(g)(1), the district court declared, was to offer mothers an opportunity to remain outside the work force in order to concentrate on child raising. Denying insurance benefits to unwed mothers of illegitimate children, the court declared, unjustifiably deprived the latter of motherly attention solely because of their status at birth.

Question: Does section 402(g)(1) contravene equal protection precepts incorporated in the Fifth Amendment?

Decision: No. Opinion by Justice Rehnquist. Vote: 5–4, Marshall, Brennan, White, and Blackmun dissenting.

Reasons: The district court misconceived the inspiration behind section 402(g)(1). Its architects sought to offer protection to mothers who were likely to suffer economic dislocation upon the death of a wage earner and who thereafter would be confronted with a choice between employment or full-time devotion to child rearing. Section 402(g)(1) rationally excludes from its protective ambit mothers who have never married the wage earner since they are far less likely than insured mothers to suffer significant economic losses when the wage earner dies. Although some divorced mothers are insured under the statute without proof of economic dependency, this does not render the denial of benefits to mothers of illegitimates constitutionally irrational. There is no constitutional obligation to limit a statute's beneficiaries to only those who have the status that spurred the statutory enactment.

It is contended, however, that section 402(g)(1) discriminates against illegitimates and thus must be scrutinized under more exacting equal protection standards. But the statute confers benefits on mothers, not children. The latter, including illegitimates, are eligible for child's insurance benefits. Any economic aid children receive through the payment of mother's benefits is merely incidental. In order to subject a statute to equal protection review on the basis of a classification derived from its disparate impact, "it is necessary to show that the class that is purportedly discriminated against . . . suffers significant deprivation of a benefit or imposition of a substantial burden." In this case, the incidental and largely speculative effect on illegitimates as a class attributable to section 402(g)(1) fails to justify treating the denial of benefits to unwed mothers as discrimination against illegitimate children.

Bell v. Wolfish, 441 U.S. 520 (1979)

Facts: The federal government erected the Metropolitan Correctional Center (MCC) in New York City primarily to house pretrial detainees awaiting federal criminal prosecution for periods ordinarily not exceeding sixty days. With a planned capacity of 449 and incorporating the most enlightened features of penological architecture, the MCC, shortly after its opening, replaced single bunks in many individual rooms and dormitories with double bunks to accommodate an unexpected flow of inmates.

A class action on behalf of all persons confined at the MCC, pretrial detainees and sentenced prisoners alike, was filed in federal district court. The complaint assailed the constitutionality of double bunking in individual rooms and a host of other MCC practices that limited the receipt of packages and hardcover books by inmates, subjected them to body cavity inspections following contact visits, and barred their presence during routine room inspections by MCC officials. The district court granted broad injunctive relief with respect to pretrial detainees. Since such persons are presumed innocent and detained solely to ensure their presence at trial, the court declared, any infringement of their rights, beyond those inherent in confinement, must be justified by a compelling necessity. Under this standard, the court held, constitutional due process could not countenance the MCC's double bunking in individual rooms and general prohibition against receipt of hardcover books mailed from outside the institution. In addition, the district court declared, the Fourth Amendment was affronted by MCC rules subjecting inmates to body cavity inspections following visitor contacts and forbidding their presence during routine room searches by correction officials. The court of appeals affirmed.

Question: Are the contested MCC practices and rules that circumscribe the freedoms of pretrial detainees unconstitutional?

Decision: No. Opinion by Justice Rehnquist. Vote 5–4, Stevens, Marshall, and Brennan dissenting, Powell dissenting with respect to the body cavity inspections only.

Reasons: The district court and the court of appeals relied on the "presumption of innocence" to justify employing a "compelling necessity" standard to appraise the constitutionality of double bunking. The presumption of innocence, however, is a doctrine that allocates the burden of proof in criminal trials. It has no application in ascertaining the rights of a pretrial detainee during his confinement before trial. And constitutional due process offers no foundation for scrutinizing all restrictions and discomforts experienced during pretrial detainment under a compelling necessity standard. The proper inquiry is whether such conditions "amount to punishment of the detainee" because due process proscribes punishment before a proper adjudication of guilt.

Whether a particular disability that accompanies pretrial detention constitutes "punishment" in the constitutional sense turns on a variety of considerations: whether the disability is affirmative, whether it has historically been regarded as punishment, whether a finding of *scienter* is required to invoke its application, whether retribution and deterrence are promoted by the sanction, whether the behavior to which it applies is a crime, whether a nonpunitive purpose can explain the disability, and whether the restriction is excessive in relation to the alternative purpose. Under this standard, in the absence of an express concession that a particular condition or restriction of pretrial detention was imposed as punishment, due process is satisfied if the questioned disability "is reasonably related to a legitimate governmental objective. . . ." In operating a pretrial detention facility, moreover, ensuring the appearance of detainees at trial as well as maintaining security, order, and effective management are legitimate government goals.

Judged under this framework, double bunking is easily exonerated of any due process infirmity. Double bunks are employed in rooms containing other furniture, a wash basin, and a toilet. Extended occupancy of the rooms is compelled only at night; during daytime, spacious common areas may be freely used. Nearly all of the detainees are released within sixty days. Although it may be uncomfortable, double bunking at the MCC falls far short of a constitutional violation. We emphatically reject the view that due process embraces some sort of "one man, one cell" principle.

The court of appeals also constitutionally proscribed four MCC restrictions and practices intended to maintain security and order at the facility: limiting the receipt of mailed hardcover books; barring the receipt of packages containing food or personal property; excluding inmates during routine room searches; and subjecting inmates to body cavity inspections following contact visits. Whether the court of appeals was correct turns on the application of two constitutional precepts. First, the rights of prison inmates and pretrial detainees may be circumscribed to safeguard the internal security of the confining institution. Second, prison administrators are entitled to broad deference in prophesying what policies and practices are needed to forestall threats to institutional discipline and security. This deference is accorded both because of the expertise and practical experience of prison administrators, and "because the operation of our correctional facilities is peculiarily the province of the Legislative and Executive Branches of our Government, not the Judicial."

As modified by the federal bureau of prisons and the MCC, the book rule prohibits the receipt of hardcover books by inmates unless mailed directly from publishers, book clubs, or bookstores. It was inspired by fear that hardcover books may be employed to smuggle contraband, money, drugs, and weapons, except when mailed from a nonsuspect source. It is undisputed, moreover, that hardcover books are difficult to search effectively. In addition, inmates retain full access to a host of other reading materials: softbound books, magazines, newspapers, and thousands of volumes in the MCC's general library. Finally, the rule's effects on pretrial detainees generally cease after a maximum of sixty days. In these circumstances, the rule is sustainable as a reasonable time, place, and manner regulation of First Amendment rights that is necessary to safeguard significant government interests.

The ban against the receipt of food or personal property packages was conceived as necessary to forestall smuggling of contraband and to reduce the risks of theft, gambling, and inmate conflicts caused by envy. The teaching of *Jones* v. *North Carolina Prisoners' Labor Union*, 433 U.S. 119 (1977), is that the ban survives due process scrutiny unless it is based on fears that have been "conclusively shown" to be false. No such showing was made in this case.

The exclusion of inmates during routine unannounced room searches serves twin purposes: to prevent friction between inmates and security guards; and to foreclose inmate obstruction of searches by distracting guards and moving contraband from room to room ahead of the search team. Expectations of privacy safeguarded by the Fourth Amendment, the lower courts held, were affronted by the exclusion. But even assuming pretrial detainees retain any reasonable expectations of privacy, which is questionable, given the realities of institutional confinement, they are not disturbed by the room search rule. The rule facilitates the safe and effective performance of the search, which all concede may be conducted. Permitting inmates to observe the searches may deter theft or misuse by guards, but it would not lessen the invasion of their privacy. Accordingly, the search rule is faithful to the Fourth Amendment norm of reasonableness.

MCC requires all inmates to expose their bodies for visual inspection as part of a strip search that follows every contact visit with an outsider. Body cavity searches are employed to discover and to deter the smuggling of weapons, drugs, and other contraband into the institution. Although these searches may invade realms of personal privacy protected by the Fourth Amendment, they are nevertheless "reasonable" and thus constitutional.

The test of Fourth Amendment reasonableness requires a balancing of the government need advanced by the search against the consequent invasion of personal rights. Fraught with serious security dangers, a detention facility is commonly afflicted with the smuggling of money, drugs, weapons, and other contraband. The record in this case documents inmate attempts to sneak these items into the MCC by concealment in body cavities. The significant and legitimate security interests the institution protects by cavity searches justify subordinating the privacy interests of the inmates in the constitutional balance.

The four questioned MCC security practices as applied to pretrial detainees do not constitute "punishment" and are thus free of any due process taint. They rationally advance the permissible nonpunitive objective of institutional order and security and were not intended by MCC officials as punishment. Like double bunking, therefore, the security practices pass constitutional muster.

There was a time not too long ago when the federal judiciary took a completely "hands-off" approach to the problem of prison administration. In recent years, however, these courts largely have discarded this "hands-off" attitude and have waded into this complex arena. The deplorable conditions and draconian restrictions of some of our Nation's prisons are too well known to require recounting here, and the federal courts rightly have condemned these sordid aspects of our prison systems. But many of these same courts have, in the name of the Constitution, become increasingly enmeshed in the minutiae of prison operations. . . . The inquiry of federal courts into prison management, [however], must be limited to the issue of whether a particular system violates any prohibition of the Constitution, or in the case of a federal prison, a statute. The wide range of "judgment calls" that meet constitutional and statutory requirements are confided to officials outside the Judicial Branch of Government.

Jones v. Wolf, 443 U.S. 595 (1979)

Facts: A schism in a Presbyterian church in Macon, Georgia, precipitated a dispute between quarreling factions over the ownership of church property. The church was a member church of the Presbyterian Church of the United States (PCUS) and governed by its constitution. Local presbyteries are empowered by the PCUS constitution to make initial decisions through their sessions, subject to the review and control of the higher church courts, the presbytery, synod, and general assembly. Although a majority of the local Presbyterian congregation voted to separate from the PCUS, a reviewing presbytery ruled that the minority faction constituted the true congregation. It stripped the majority faction of authority to exercise office derived from the PCUS.

Representatives of the minority faction then initiated suit in state court to obtain exclusive use and possession of the local church's property as a member congregation of the PCUS. Purporting to apply "neutral principles of law," the trial court granted judgment for the majority faction. The Supreme Court of Georgia affirmed, rejecting the claim that its ruling violated the First Amendment's protection of religious freedom.

Question: Does the First Amendment proscribe civil court resolution of church property disputes pursuant to neutral principles of law?

Decision: No. Opinion by Justice Blackmun. Vote: 5–4, Powell, Burger, Stewart, and White dissenting.

Reasons: Civil courts are precluded under the First Amendment from resolving church property disputes on the basis of religious doctrine and practice. They cannot review decisions of the highest court of a hierarchical church organization relating to religious doctrine or policy. But civil courts may resolve litigation over church property by invoking "neutral principles of law" that eschew any inquiry into doctrinal matters, such as ritual and liturgy of worship or the tenets of faith. The neutral principles approach must rely exclusively on objective, well-established concepts of trust and property law. It thereby avoids any secular intrusion on religious freedom.

Through appropriate reversionary clauses and trust provisions, religious societies can specify what is to happen to church property in the event of a particular contingency, or what religious body will determine the ownership in the event of a schism or doctrinal controversy. In this manner, a religious organization can ensure that a dispute over the ownership of church property will be resolved in accord with the desires of the members.

The Georgia Supreme Court, however, failed to apply neutral principles of law in a constitutional fashion to resolve the church property dispute in this case. It unreflectively assumed that local Presbyterian churches are represented by the majority. The First Amendment does not prevent a state from embracing a presumptive rule of majority representation, capable of being annulled upon a showing that the identity of the local church is to be determined by some other means. Under this neutral principles approach, the presumptive rule could be overcome "either by providing, in the corporate charter or the constitution of the general church, that the identity of the local church is to be established in some other way, or by providing that the church property is held in trust for the general church and those who remain loyal to it." Since the Georgia Supreme Court failed to articulate neutral principles of law for recognizing the majority faction as representative of the local presbytery, however, the case must be remanded for further exposition of its decision.

Califano v. Aznavorian, 439 U.S. 170 (1978)

Facts: Section 1611(f) of the Social Security Act temporarily terminates benefits to otherwise qualified aged, blind, or disabled persons if they are outside the United States for all of any month. The termination extends until the recipient resumes residence in the United States for thirty consecutive days. A federal district court held that section 1611(f) unconstitutionally chilled the right of international travel. The statute's temporary revocation of benefits, it declared, was insufficiently related to the government's interest in confining payments solely to bona fide residents to survive constitutional scrutiny.

Question: Does section 1611(f) place an impermissible burden on the constitutional right of international travel?

Decision: No. Opinion by Justice Stewart. Vote: 9–0.

Reasons: Generally speaking, classifications drawn in social welfare legislation are invulnerable to constitutional attack if they have a rational basis. No different standard of constitutional scrutiny is called for simply because a classification may incidentally inhibit the exercise of the right of international travel. Unlike the right of interstate travel, the right to travel abroad has never been viewed as fundamental in the hierarchy of constitutionally protected freedoms.

Section 1611(f) rationally advances the legitimate statutory goal of confining benefits to bona fide residents of the United States. The legislative choice to permit resumption of benefits to an international traveler only after thirty days' consecutive residence in the United States adds assurance that the residence is genuine. In addition, section 1611(f) may have been embraced to avoid the difficulties of monitoring a beneficiary's continuing eligibility outside the country and to encourage the expenditure of social security payments in the United States. These justifications are sufficiently rational to absolve section 1611(f) of the asserted constitutional infirmity.

Southeastern Community College v. *Davis,* 442 U.S. 397 (1979)

Facts: An applicant for a nursing program offered by a state community college was denied admission because of a serious hearing disability. The disability prevented her from understanding normal spoken speech and precluded safe participation in the normal clinical training program, where lipreading was impossible or impracticable. The applicant challenged the legality of her exclusion from the nursing program under section 504 of the Rehabilitation Act of 1973. That section prohibits discrimination against an "otherwise qualified handicapped individual" in federally funded programs "solely by reasons of his handicap." (The state community college concededly received federal funds.)

The district court entered judgment in favor of the college. The applicant was not "otherwise qualified" for the college's nursing program within the meaning of section 504, it found, because her hearing disability would prevent her from safely performing clinical training tasks and work required of registered nurses. Reversing, the court of appeals held that section 504 obliged the college to evaluate the applicant's qualifications for its nursing program without regard to her hearing disability.

Question: Did the college violate section 504 by denying an applicant admission to its nursing program because of her hearing impairment?

Decision: No. Unanimous opinion by Justice Powell.

Reasons: The language of a statute is the starting point for its interpretation. Section 504 by its terms does not compel educational institutions either to close their eyes to handicaps that limit the capacities of individuals or to accommodate such disabilities by substantially modifying their programs. Instead, its language suggests only a prohibition against unreflective assumptions that the mere possession of a handicap disables an individual from performing adequately in a particular context.

It is undisputed that the ability to understand speech without reliance on lipreading is necessary for full participation in the college's nursing program and to function effectively as a registered nurse. The applicant's exclusion from the program was founded on her inability to satisfy reasonable physical qualifications, not on unthinking prejudice against handicapped persons that section 504 proscribes.

The applicant contends, however, that section 504 requires affirmative action to accommodate the special needs of the handicapped. Individual supervision by faculty members, dispensing with certain required courses, and training for only some of the tasks required by licensed registered nurses, the applicant maintains, would permit her enrollment in the college's nursing program. But neither the language, purpose, nor history of section 504 can support imposing such a formidable affirmative action obligation on recipients of federal funds.

The line between a lawful refusal to extend affirmative action and illegal discrimination against handicapped persons may at times be dim. A refusal to modify an existing program might become unreasonable and discriminatory. In this case, however, the applicant could not participate in the nursing program unless the standards were substantially lowered.

> Section 504 imposes no requirement upon an educational institution to lower or to effect substantial modification of standards to accommodate a handicapped person.

School Desegregation

The Court grappled twice with school desegregation controversies that emerged from northern public school systems with no history of racial separation imposed by statute. In *Columbus Board of Education v. Penick*, 443 U.S. 449 (1979), a 7–2 majority upheld a finding that purposeful, racially discriminatory actions of a board of education had infected the entire school system and therefore justified a systemwide remedial decree. Writing for the Court, Justice White asserted that a combination of racially inspired board action and current pronounced segregation authorizes a systemwide remedy, unless the board can show that part of the current imbalance cannot be ascribed to the constitutional breach. The Court further expounded the circumstances justifying a systemwide desegregation decree in *Dayton Board of Education* v. *Brinkman*, 443 U.S. 526 (1979). Voting 5–4 to sustain a systemwide decree in Dayton, Ohio, the Court declared that intentional racial discrimination in a substantial part of a school system supports an inference of systemwide discriminatory intent. That constitutionally objectionable intent, the Court maintained, could justify an inference that racial separation throughout the school system resulted from unconstitutional actions.

Columbus Board of Education v. *Penick*, 443 U.S. 449 (1979)

Facts: In 1973, a complaint was filed in federal district court alleging that the public schools of Columbus, Ohio, were unconstitutionally segregated. After a lengthy trial, the district court sustained the complaint and ordered the implementation of a systemwide school desegregation plan. The public schools were openly and intentionally racially segregated, the district court found, when *Brown* v. *Board of Education*, 347 U.S. 483 (1954), held legally mandated racial separation unconstitutional. The court further found that the Columbus board of education had subsequently failed to dismantle its dual system and had acted in several ways to reinforce racial segregation within the public school system. Accordingly, it held that a systemwide desegregation remedy was necessary to rectify the effects of the board's racially inspired actions. The court of appeals affirmed.

Question: Did the lower courts err in finding that segregation in the Columbia public schools could be ascribed to intentional racially discriminatory actions by the board of education and in ordering a systemwide desegregation remedy?

Decision: No. Opinion by Justice White. Vote: 7–2, Powell and Rehnquist dissenting.

Reasons: The board contends that the findings of intentional segregative conduct were clearly erroneous and thus no constitutional violation was proved. It notes that segregated schooling was not commanded by state law when *Brown* was decided. The district court found, however, that official acts of the board animated by racial considerations were the cause of segregation in a substantial part of the school system. This finding was justified by the evidence and the demonstrated existence of unconstitutional segregation in 1954.

Local school boards are charged with an affirmative duty to dismantle racially segregated school systems that go contrary to constitutional norms. The Columbus school board had both failed to discharge this obligation at the time of trial and had intentionally increased racial segregation since 1954 through use of optional attendance zones, noncontiguous attendance areas, boundary changes, and school site selection. In addition, the district court found, and the court of appeals affirmed, that the board's intentional segregative action had a current systemwide effect that necessitated a systemwide remedy. Without reason to disturb this finding, the need for a systemwide remedy is unassailable. A fundamental teaching of *Keyes* v. *School Dist. No. 1*, 413 U.S. 189 (1973), and *Swann* v. *Charlotte-Mecklenburg Board of Education*, 402 U.S. 1 (1971), is that racially inspired official action coupled with pronounced current segregation authorizes a systemwide remedy, unless there is a showing by the board specifying what part of the current imbalance was not attributable to the constitutional breach. In this case, the board failed to dispel the evidence of systemwide impact and was properly charged with effecting a suitable remedy.

Dayton Board of Education v. Brinkman, 443 U.S. 526 (1979)

Facts: In 1972, a complaint was filed in federal district court alleging that the public schools of Dayton, Ohio, were unconstitutionally segregated. After protracted litigation and several appeals, the district court dismissed the complaint. Conceding that Dayton's schools were marked by conspicuous racial imbalance, the district court nevertheless exonerated the local board of education of any constitutional liability. The current racial separation, it found, was not the result of any intentionally discriminatory or other actions of the board. The court of appeals reversed. At the time of *Brown* v. *Board of Education*, 347 U.S. 483 (1954), the court declared, the board was operating a racially discriminatory school system that it was constitutionally obligated to dismantle, that it had defaulted on this obligation, and that this default coupled with the intentionally segregative effect of various practices since 1954 had systemwide consequences and justified systemwide relief.

Question: Did the court of appeals correctly conclude that the board was operating a racially segregated school system in 1954 and that the current effects of its intentionally discriminatory actions justified a systemwide desegregation decree?

Decision: Yes. Opinion by Justice White. Vote: 5–4, Stewart, Burger, Powell, and Rehnquist dissenting.

Reasons: The record offered substantial support for the finding of the court of appeals that in 1954 intentionally discriminatory actions by the board were responsible for conspicuous racial imbalance in the public schools. This constitutional breach created a duty on the part of the board to eradicate the effects of its racially discriminatory conduct. The court of appeals found, however, that the board had repeatedly failed to discharge its duty since 1954 and in some instances had acted purposely to perpetuate racial separation. Nothing in the record would justify upsetting these findings. Finally, the court of appeals inferred that current systemwide segregation was the product of past intentionally discriminatory actions and authorized a systemwide remedy. The inference was faithful to the holding in *Columbus Board of Education* v. *Penick,* 443 U.S. 449 (1979) that

> purposeful discrimination in a substantial part of a school system furnishes a sufficient basis for an inferential finding of a systemwide discriminatory intent unless otherwise rebutted, and that given the purpose to operate a dual school system one could infer a connection between such a purpose and racial separation in other parts of the school system.

Abortion

The constitutional jurisprudence of abortion evolved by the Burger Court exhibits a pronounced disrespect for the legislative process[1]

---

[1] Compare Planned Parenthood of Central Missouri v. Danforth, 428 U.S. 52 (1976) (rejecting a legislative finding that a prohibition on employing saline amniocentesis as a method of abortion after the first trimester of pregnancy is reasonably related to maternal health), with Massachusetts Board of Retirement v. Murgia, 427 U.S. 307 (1976) (respecting a legislative decision to require all uniformed state police officers to retire at age 50).

and for traditional family roles,[2] even though it has repeatedly championed such values elsewhere. In 1973, the Court sharply curtailed the authority of states to restrict abortions in the landmark decisions rendered in *Roe* v. *Wade*, 410 U.S. 113 (1973), and *Doe* v. *Bolton*, 410 U.S. 179 (1973). Three fundamental teachings emerged from these cases: during the first trimester of pregnancy, an adult woman is constitutionally entitled to obtain an abortion from a willing physician; during the second trimester, the state may regulate the abortion procedure in furtherance of maternal health but may not override the abortion choice; and during the last trimester of pregnancy, the state may proscribe abortion, except when necessary to preserve the physical or psychological health of the mother. The lofty constitutional status of the abortion choice was reinforced in *Bigelow* v. *Virginia*, 421 U.S. 809 (1975). There the Court bestowed First Amendment blessing on a newspaper advertisement informing Virginia residents where legal abortions in New York could be obtained.[3]

Family concerns bowed to the abortion choice in *Planned Parenthood of Central Missouri* v. *Danforth*, 428 U.S. 52 (1976). There the Court declared unconstitutional statutory provisions investing a husband with authority to veto the abortion decision of his wife during the first trimester of pregnancy and investing parents with authority to veto the abortion decision of their minor children during this period. Writing for the Court, Justice Blackmun insisted that the invalidated provisions would not foster family harmony and unity. A provision proscribing the use of saline amniocentesis as an abortion method also evoked the Court's opposition in *Planned Parenthood*. The Court immersed itself in medical disputation and declared that the proscription was not reasonably related to protecting maternal health. Accordingly, the Court held, the impediment to abortion created by the proscription could not be defended constitutionally.

The Court was less solicitous of the constitutional right to an abortion in *Maher* v. *Roe*, 432 U.S. 464 (1977) and *Poelker* v. *Doe*, 432 U.S. 519 (1977). Equal protection tenets, the Court declared, do not prohibit states from subsidizing childbirth and medically necessary abortions, while refusing to underwrite nontherapeutic abortions.

---

[2] Compare Planned Parenthood of Central Missouri v. Danforth, supra, n. 1 (holding unconstitutional state statute empowering parents to override abortion decision made by minor children), with Parham v. J. R., 442 U.S. 84 (1979) (acknowledging broad parental power to seek commitment of minor children to state-operated mental health hospitals), and FCC v. Pacifica Foundation, 438 U.S. 726 (1978) (recognizing a legitimate parental interest in shielding their children from indecent speech or material).
[3] Specifically, the Court invalidated a criminal conviction against a newspaper for publishing the advertisement.

The 1978–1979 term, however, witnessed renewed support of abortion rights. In *Bellotti* v. *Baird*, 443 U.S. 622 (1979), the Court invalidated a statute that required unmarried minors younger than age eighteen to consult with their parents before seeking an abortion. The Court further held that empowering a judge to override the abortion decision of a mature minor upon a finding that an abortion would conflict with her best interests was constitutionally intolerable. And speaking for a 6–3 majority in *Colautti* v. *Franklin*, 439 U.S. 379 (1979), Justice Blackmun inveighed against a statute making it a crime for a physician who performs an abortion to desist from seeking to preserve the life of the fetus if it is either "viable" or there is "sufficient reason to believe that [it] may be viable." The statute, Blackmun stated, was unconstitutionally vague.

Bellotti v. *Baird*, 443 U.S. 622 (1979)

Facts: A Massachusetts statute imposed modest restrictions on the right of unmarried minors (less than eighteen years of age) to obtain an abortion. The consent of both parents is ordinarily required to legalize an abortion operation on a minor. If parental consent is refused, however, a minor may obtain judicial authorization for an abortion if the parents are notified of the proceeding and the court finds that an abortion would be in the minor's best interest. Prompt appellate review of a court finding is assured under conditions that maintain the confidentiality of the names of the minor and her parents. A three-judge federal district court invalidated the statute, concluding that its constitutional infirmities were threefold. The statutory insistence that parental permission be sought or notice given by minors whose best interests would be served by acting otherwise, the court declared, placed an impermissible burden on the right to seek an abortion. In addition, the court asserted, a judge could not constitutionally be empowered to veto an abortion decision of a minor found capable of giving informed consent. Finally, the court ruled that the statutory failure explicitly to inform parents that consent could be withheld only to promote the minor's best interests would unconstitutionally precipitate wrongful refusals.

Question: Does the Massachusetts statute unconstitutionally burden the right to obtain an abortion by empowering judges to overrule abortion decisions made by mature and competent minors and by requiring that they consult or notify their parents before obtaining an abortion?

135

Decision: Yes. Plurality opinion by Justice Powell. Vote: 8–1, White dissenting, Stevens, Brennan, Marshall, and Blackmun concurring.

Reasons: The constitutional rights of children do not mirror those of adults. This doctrine is bottomed on the peculiar vulnerability of minors, their inability to make critical decisions in an informed, mature manner, and the cardinal parental role in child rearing. Ordinarily, a state may broadly curtail the choices of minors over matters necessitating special protection to fortify the parental role. The unique nature of the abortion decision and its preferred constitutional status, however, necessitates curtailing the state's power over minors in this matter. The education, employment skills, financial resources, and emotional maturity of pregnant minors would frequently make unwanted motherhood an ordeal carrying grave and ineradicable consequences. We thus conclude that a state may not require a pregnant minor to obtain parental consent to an abortion without offering an alternative method for obtaining the requisite authorization. The alternative procedure must permit the minor to show either

> that she is mature enough and well enough informed to make her abortion decision, in consultation with her physician, independently of her parents' wishes; or . . . that even if she is not able to make this decision independently, the desired abortion would be in her best interests. The proceeding in which this showing is made must assure that a resolution of the issue, and any appeals that may follow, will be completed with anonymity and sufficient expedition to provide an effective opportunity for an abortion to be obtained.

Measured by these constitutional standards, the contested statute is twice flawed. Although it offers minors a judicial procedure for sanctioning an abortion when parents withhold consent, the obligation of prior parental notice will frequently frustrate access to a court. Many objecting parents will hold strong views against abortion and can employ a variety of tactics to discourage their vulnerable offspring from obtaining judicial approval. A minor is constitutionally entitled, therefore, to go directly to court without consulting or notifying her parents. Approval for a requested abortion must be forthcoming unless the judge is persuaded both that the minor is immature and that an abortion would be contrary to her best interests. The nurturing of family bonds and the parental role in child rearing may be considered by the judge in determining whether an abortion would further the best interests of the pregnant minor.

[T]he court may deny the abortion request of an immature minor in the absence of parental consultation if it concludes that her best interests would be served thereby, or the court may in such a case defer decision until there is parental consultation in which the court may participate.

The contested statute also bestows authority on judges to veto the abortion decisions of minors who are found mature and competent. This authority unconstitutionally constricts the abortion choices of mature minors.

Colautti v. *Franklin,* **439 U.S. 379 (1979)**

Facts: Section 5 of the Pennsylvania Abortion Control Act makes it a crime for a physician who performs an abortion to fail to seek preservation of the life of the fetus if it is either "viable" or there is "sufficient reason to believe that [it] may be viable." Specifically, if either of the latter conditions exist, the physician must exercise the same care to preserve the life and health of the fetus as is required when a fetus is intended to be born alive and must employ the abortion technique that maximizes the fetus's opportunity for survival, unless a different technique is necessary to preserve the life or health of the mother. A three-judge federal district court invalidated section 5 on the ground, among others, that it was unconstitutionally vague.

Question: Is section 5 unconstitutionally vague?

Decision: Yes. Opinion by Justice Blackmun. Vote: 6–3, White, Burger, and Rehnquist dissenting.

Reasons: Due process condemns criminal statutes that fail to offer fair warning of what conduct is forbidden or are conducive to arbitrary arrests and convictions because their prohibitory ambit is so foggy. Section 5 is infected with both vices.

It obligates a physician performing an abortion to adhere to a prescribed standard of care if he determines that the fetus "is viable," or if "there is sufficient reason to believe that the fetus may be viable." Whether the presence of the latter condition is to be determined solely with reference to the subjective belief of the attending physician, or with reference to the beliefs of a cross section of the medical community or a panel of experts, however, is uncertain. The phrase "may be viable" enhances this uncertainty. To construe it as synonymous with the word "viable" would violate elementary canons of statutory construction. Its ambiguity permits an interpretation that refers to an exclusive time period during pregnancy when there is a remote possibility of fetal survival outside the womb, but when the fetus has not yet attained the reasonable likelihood of survival that physicians associate with viability. The vagueness problems with section 5 are compounded by its imposition of criminal liability without regard to fault by the attending physician. That is, a physician confronts the prospect of criminal conviction because of an erroneous, albeit good faith determination that a fetus was not viable at the time of abortion. Accordingly, section 5 is void for vagueness. It is unnecessary to decide whether a finding of bad faith or some other type of *scienter* is a constitutional prerequisite for holding a physician criminally accountable for an erroneous assessment of viability.

Section 5 is also constitutionally tainted because it prescribes a standard of care that is riddled with uncertainty. It obligates a physician to employ abortion techniques offering the greatest possibility of fetal survival so long as the life or health of the mother would not be endangered. There is professional disagreement, however, about the relative merits and safety of abortion techniques that may be employed during the second trimester of pregnancy. These techniques include saline amnioinfusion, prostaglandin infusion, hysterotomy, and oxytosin induction. It is not clear, moreover, whether the interest in the fetus's life and health must in all circumstances be subordinated to concerns about the mother in the choice of an abortion technique. Section 5 may obligate the physician to sacrifice a margin of safety for the mother to increase the probability of fetal survival. This uncertainty is exacerbated by the lack of any *scienter* requirement.

> [W]here conflicting duties of this magnitude are involved, the State, at the least, must proceed with greater precision before it may subject a physician to possible criminal sanctions.

Federal Courts and Procedure

Questions of abstention, justiciability, standing, and collateral estoppel highlighted a group of decisions dealing with federal courts. The Court chastized a district judge for failing to abstain from examining the constitutionality of a host of Texas family code provisions in *Moore v. Sims*, 442 U.S. 415 (1979). The abstention doctrine expounded in *Younger* v. *Harris*, 401 U.S. 37 (1971), and its sequel, Justice Rehnquist declared for a 5–4 majority, generally rules out concurrent federal adjudication of constitutional issues that can be raised by the federal plaintiff in a pending state criminal proceeding or civil suit seeking to safeguard important state interests. In *Moore,* Rehnquist noted, the federal plaintiffs could have raised their constitutional challenges in a pending state suit seeking to curtail their authority and control over an allegedly battered child. Simply because a constitutional challenge is lodged against a broad, complex statutory scheme or emerges from a child custody dispute, Rehnquist asserted, affords no reason for discarding the *Younger* presumption favoring abstention. The *Moore* decision reflects a yawning and seemingly irresistible extension of *Younger* principles to civil litigation initiated by states.[1]

A federal district court was also rebuked for prematurely entertaining constitutional questions in *Babbitt* v. *United Farm Workers National Union,* 442 U.S. 289 (1979). Two issues adjudicated were nonjusticiable, the Court declared, since any injury threatened by the assailed statutes lay in the realm of conjecture. And three other constitutional questions, the Court noted, might be avoided or modified by a definitive resolution of ambiguous state statutes in state courts. Accordingly, the Court concluded, the district court should have abstained to await their interpretation.

In contrast to staunch opposition against assertions of standing displayed in some prior decisions,[2] the Court assumed a benevolent approach in *Gladstone, Realtors* v. *Village of Bellwood,* 441 U.S. 91 (1979). There a 7–2 majority interpreted section 812 of the Fair Housing Act to confer standing as broad as that constitutionally permissible. In addition, the Court held that alleged economic and community injuries to a village and alleged deprivation of social and professional opportunities associated with residency in an integrated neighborhood were sufficient to confer standing to attack unlawful "racial steering" in the housing market.

The Court expounded on the doctrine of collateral estoppel in two cases. An 8–1 majority ruled that the doctrine may be wielded by a federal plaintiff to prevent a defendant from relitigating issues of fact adjudicated adversely to that defendant in prior litigation. The

---

[1] See Huffman v. Pursue, Ltd., 420 U.S. 592 (1975) (Younger applicable to public nuisance suit seeking closure of a theater that exhibited obscene films); Judice v. Vail, 430 U.S. 327 (1977) (Younger applicable to state civil contempt proceedings); Trainor v. Hernandez, 431 U.S. 434 (1977) (Younger applicable to state proceedings seeking recovery of welfare payments allegedly obtained by fraud).

[2] See, for example, Warth v. Seldon, 422 U.S. 490 (1975); Simon v. Eastern Kentucky Welfare Rights Organization, 426 U.S. 26 (1976); Laird v. Tatum, 408 U.S. 1 (1972); United States v. Richardson, 418 U.S. 166 (1974); Linda R. S. v. Richard D., 410 U.S. 614 (1973).

Seventh Amendment right of jury trial in civil cases, the Court maintained, was not disturbed by this augmentation of collateral estoppel principles (*Parklane Hosiery Co., Inc.* v. *Shore*, 439 U.S. 322 [1979]). The Court also held that collateral estoppel was an insurmountable barrier to a federal government suit in federal court assailing the constitutionality of a state tax levied on federal contractors that had previously been absolved of the claimed infirmity in state litigation (*Montana* v. *United States*, 440 U.S. 147 [1979]).

Rule 6(e) of the Federal Rules of Criminal Procedure empowers a district court to disclose grand jury materials to an applicant only upon a showing of "particularized need." Several distinct interests are preserved by continued secrecy: encouraging full and fearless testimony from witnesses, forestalling improper influence of grand jurors or flight by a suspect, and protecting the good name of a grand jury target found innocent. Lifting the curtain on grand jury proceedings under Rule 6(e) is proper only when the need outweighs the public interest in continued secrecy. A cumbersome, two-part procedure for making this determination was endorsed in *Douglas Oil Co. of California* v. *Petrol Stops Northwest*, 441 U.S. 211 (1979), where the requested grand jury materials were to be used in a district court different from the one that had supervised the grand jury. The supervisory court should make an initial evaluation of the need for continued secrecy, the Court concluded, and then send the requested materials to the district court in which their use was wanted for an appraisal of the applicant's litigating needs.

Finally, the Court held that appeal rather than mandamus was the proper route for challenging the validity of an indictment of a congressman on the ground that it offended the legislative speech or debate clause immunity of Article I, Section 6, clause 1 of the Constitution (*Helstoski* v. *Meanor*, 442 U.S. 500 [1979]).

Moore v. *Sims*, 442 U.S. 415 (1979)

Facts: With evidence of child battering, the Texas Department of Human Resources obtained an ex parte emergency order giving it temporary custody of an elementary school student. Thereafter, the parents moved in state court to terminate the department's temporary custody, and the department sued the parents under the Texas family code seeking to curtail their authority and control over the child. The parents countered by filing suit in federal district court assailing the constitutionality of several interrelated provisions of the family code. After the state's temporary custody order had expired, the federal district court enjoined the complementary state proceeding affecting the parent-child relationship and held several provisions of the family code unconstitutional. Abstention under the doctrine of *Younger* v. *Harris*, 401 U.S. 37 (1971), was unwarranted, the district court declared, because the federal suit was multifaceted, involved custody of children, and was the offspring of procedural confusion in state courts.

Question: Did the federal district court violate the abstention doctrine expounded in *Younger* v. *Harris* and its progeny by enjoining the state's parent-child relationship suit and ruling on the constitutionality of a host of family code provisions?

Decision: Yes. Opinion by Justice Rehnquist. Vote: 5–4, Stevens, Brennan, Stewart, and Marshall dissenting.

Reasons: The *Younger* doctrine counsels federal court abstention when there are pending state criminal proceedings or civil proceedings seeking to safeguard important state interests where the federal plaintiff may present his constitutional claims. Federal intervention in these ongoing state proceedings is permissible only when necessary to rescue the federal plaintiff from great and immediate irreparable injury. And a harm of that magnitude generally can be demonstrated only by proof that the state proceeding was conceived in bad faith or was initiated pursuant to a flagrantly unconstitutional statute.

In this case, the enjoined state proceeding seeking the temporary removal of a child because of suspected battering implicated state concerns of sufficient moment to invoke the *Younger* doctrine of abstention. The federal plaintiffs had the opportunity to present their constitutional challenges in the state forum, either by counterclaim or otherwise. None of the reasons advanced by the federal district court justified its departure from the *Younger* presumption favoring absention.

The breadth of the constitutional challenge to a complex state statutory scheme, the district court opined, militated against absention. That viewpoint, however, misconceives abstention precepts— which seek to forestall federal interference with sensitive areas of state social or economic policy. The broader the constitutional challenges and the more complex the statutory scheme assailed, the greater the need to respect state resolution of the issues in the first instances. This deference avoids erroneous construction of state law and limits constitutional adjudication to state statutes causing concrete injury to the federal plaintiff.

The district court seemed to equate the procedural confusion in state courts with the bad faith exception to *Younger*. But the confusion was created by a new and complex statutory scheme, not by any bad faith motives of state authorities.

Finally, the district court indicated that the extraordinary circumstance of a child custody dispute justified discarding the *Younger* presumption championing abstention. The allegedly abused child, however, was in parental custody when the federal injunction against further state proceedings was issued. The parents, moreover, had a state forum to defend against the state's quest for the child's temporary custody. There is no foundation for placing all state proceedings seeking to protect allegedly abused children outside the protective shield of *Younger*. "We are unwilling to conclude that state processes are unequal to the task of accommodating the various interests and deciding the constitutional questions that may arise in child welfare litigation."

Babbitt v. *United Farm Workers National Union*, 442 U.S. 289 (1979)

Facts: The United Farm Workers National Union (UFW) brought suit assailing the constitutionality of several provisions of the Arizona Agricultural Employment Relations Act. A three-judge federal district court invalidated provisions governing union election procedures for agricultural employees, curtailing union publicity aimed at consumers of agricultural products, exacting criminal penalties for violating the act, relieving employers of any obligation to assist union organizers in communicating with their employees, and mandating compulsory arbitration of disputes that precipitate strikes or boycotts. On appeal, the U.S. Supreme Court raised the question whether the district court should have declined from addressing the merits of the constitutional claims presented.

Question: Did the district court err in deciding the merits of the constitutional challenges to the act?

Decision: Yes, except for the provision governing union elections, which was erroneously invalidated. Opinion by Justice White. Vote: 7–2, Brennan and Marshall dissenting in part.

Reasons: Article III of the Constitution delimits the jurisdiction of of federal courts to justiciable disputes. A controversy is justiciable only if the plaintiff alleges actual or threatened concrete injury ascribable to the statute or conduct he is assailing. The constitutional attack on the provision governing the access of union organizers to an employer's agricultural employees was nonjusticiable because it failed to satisfy the concrete injury requirement. Although the provision relieves employers of any obligation to grant the UFW access to their property in order to communicate with farm workers residing there, whether access will be denied by particular employers is at present in the domain of prophecy. This uncertainty is fatal to the constitutional attack since it is bottomed on the analogy of farm labor camps to the company town in *Marsh* v. *Alabama*, 326 U.S. 501 (1946), held subject to the First Amendment. Whether access will be denied to these types of labor camps is conjectural. The constitutional challenge to the access provision must await such time as the UFW can assert an interest in seeking access to particular facilities coupled with a palpable basis for believing that access will be refused.

The dispute over the compulsory arbitration provision also was not justiciable. Its application is triggered only if an employer seeks a temporary restraining order to enjoin an unlawful strike. But whether an unlawful strike will occur and whether an employer will elect a judicial response among a host of other tactics is speculative. Any ruling on the compulsory arbitration provision, therefore, would be wholly advisory and outside the ambit of the federal judicial power.

The doctrine of abstention required deferring resolution of the constitutional challenges to the criminal penalty and consumer publicity provisions of the act until they have been authoritatively construed by Arizona state courts. This conclusion follows from the precept that counsels federal restraint where the challenged state statute is fairly susceptible of a construction by the state judiciary that would avoid or modify the necessity of reaching a federal constitutional question.

The criminal penalty was held unconstitutionally vague because of the perceived ambiguous scope of its prohibitive ambit. Arizona courts, however, might reasonably place a narrowing or illuminating construction on the penalty provision in a single proceeding and thereby obviate or modify the vagueness attack.

The constitutional challenges to the publicity provision might also be affected by state court clarification of several ambiguities. The provision was held offensive to the First Amendment on the theory that innocent or negligent misrepresentations communicated by labor organizations to consumers was prohibited. But a plausible alternative construction would proscribe only misrepresentations inspired by malice, which would sharply modify the First Amendment question presented. The district court should have abstained to await resolution of the ambiguity in Arizona courts.

The district court also held that the consumer publicity provision unconstitutionally precluded publicity aimed at products of employers not involved in a primary dispute with the labor organization. A reasonable alternative interpretation of the provision, however, is that no such proscription was intended. Another plausible construction is that only expressions carrying a threat of force are prohibited. The district court should not have entertained the challenge to the consumer publicity section without the benefit of an authoritative construction by the Arizona courts.

The union election provision was properly entertained but incorrectly overturned on the ground that it violated the freedom of association safeguarded by the First Amendment. The delays assertedly attending the procedures for choosing a collective bargaining agent and the restrictions on eligibility to vote, the district court declared, infringed on the constitutional liberty to form a labor union. The First Amendment, however, does not oblige employers to negotiate collectively with employees. Any such obligation arises only by statute. The statutory procedures that employees must pursue to designate a bargaining agent and to compel an employer to negotiate are, therefore, outside the ambit of the First Amendment.

Gladstone, Realtors v. *Village of Bellwood,* 441 U.S. 91 (1979)

Facts: Four white residents of Bellwood, Illinois, and one black resident of neighboring Maywood contacted two real estate brokerage firms with the undisclosed purpose of determining whether they practiced "racial steering," that is, directing prospective home buyers interested in equivalent properties to separate areas according to their race. The residents were not in fact interested in purchasing homes in the general Bellwood area, although they said they were. The four Bellwood residents along with the Village of Bellwood filed suit in federal district court against the realtors under section 812 of the 1968 Fair Housing Act. Prospective black buyers, the complaint alleged, were steered toward homes in an integrated area of Bellwood approximately twelve by thirteen blocks in dimension. White customers, in contrast, were allegedly steered toward homes in predominantly white areas. The allegedly unlawful racial steering had injured the Village of Bellwood, the complaint added, by manipulating the housing market to the economic and social detriment of its citizens. And the racial steering had caused the individual plaintiffs injury, it was alleged, by depriving them of the social and professional benefits of living in an integrated community.

The district court granted summary judgment for the realtors. Section 812 of the act, the court ruled, protects only "direct victims" of racially discriminatory housing practices. Since the individual plaintiffs had acted only as "testers" and not as bona fide prospective home buyers, the court declared they lacked standing to rectify section 812 violations. Reversing, the court of appeals held that section 812 protects residents against the loss of social and professional opportunities that accompany an integrated society. Thus, it reasoned, the individual plaintiffs had standing to maintain the section 812 action, even if their injuries flowed only indirectly from the discriminatory acts challenged. The court of appeals also rejected the argument that the alleged injuries to the village and the individuals were too vague and indistinct to make out a case or controversy within the federal judicial power as circumscribed by Article III of the Constitution.

Question: Did the Village of Bellwood and the individual plaintiffs have statutory and constitutional standing to attack the alleged practices of racial steering under section 812 of the act?

Decision: Yes. Opinion by Justice Powell. Vote: 7–2, Rehnquist and Stewart dissenting.

Reasons: In *Trafficante* v. *Metropolitan Life Insurance Co.*, 409 U.S. 205 (1972), the Court held that section 810 of the act, which requires that administrative remedies be exhausted by claimants injured by discriminatory housing practices, conferred standing "as broa[d] as is permitted by Article III of the Constitution." Although administrative exhaustion is not mandated by section 812, its terms and legislative history compel the conclusion that it confers standing coextensive with that constitutionally permissible.

To satisfy the standing requirements of Article III, "the plaintiff must show that he personally has suffered some actual or threatened injury as a result of the putatively illegal conduct of the defendant." In this case, the complaint alleged that the questioned racial steering practices threatened injury to the Village of Bellwood by displacing an integrated neighborhood with a segregated one, reducing property values and diminishing the village tax base, and bringing on other harms endemic to segregated communities, such as segregated schooling. If these allegations of injury are substantiated the village has standing to challenge the legality of the racial steering.

The four individual plaintiffs reside within that integrated neighborhood of Bellwood that is allegedly the target of racial steering. Their alleged injuries ascribable to the steering consist of reduced home values and the loss of social and professional benefits associated with an integrated neighborhood. The latter injuries mirror those recognized as constitutionally cognizable in *Trafficante*, where black and white apartment residents complained that the landlord's exclusion of nonwhites from the complex deprived them of the social and professional advantages of living in an integrated community. "[F]or the purpose of standing analysis, we perceive no categorical distinction between injury from racial steering suffered by occupants of a large apartment complex and that imposed upon residents of a relatively compact neighborhood such as Bellwood." Of course, some neighborhoods may be so large, heavily or sparsely populated, or so lacking in shared social and commercial activity that racial steering would inflict no actual injury to a particular resident. The presence of genuine injury, however, is a question of fact that should be determined at trial. A complaint should not be dismissed simply because actual injury might not subsequently be demonstrated. Accordingly, the individual deprivations of social and professional opportunities alleged in the complaint and illuminated by initial discovery were sufficient to withstand the defendants' motion for summary judgment.

The allegations of depreciated home values caused by the racial steering were also clearly sufficient under Article III to grant standing to contest its legality.

Parklane Hosiery Co., Inc. v. *Shore,* 439 U.S. 322 (1979)

Facts: Seeking damages and cancellation or the setting aside of a merger, a class action suit was brought against a corporation and several of its officers, directors, and stockholders for allegedly violating the Securities Exchange Act of 1934 by issuing a materially false and misleading proxy statement in connection with the merger. Before the private action came to trial, the Securities and Exchange Commission brought suit against the same defendants in federal district court alleging legal defects in the proxy statement that mirrored those alleged in the private suit. After a bench trial, the district judge found that the proxy statement was materially false and misleading and issued a declaratory judgment in favor of the commission. The private plaintiffs then moved for partial summary judgment, urging that the doctrine of collateral estoppel prevented the defendants from relitigating the issues that had been resolved against them in the commission's successful suit. The district court denied the motion, reasoning that the Seventh Amendment right to jury trial protected the defendants against such an application of collateral estoppel. The court of appeals reversed, holding that a party who has had issues of fact determined against him after a full and fair opportunity to litigate in a nonjury trial is collaterally estopped from demanding a subsequent jury trial of these same issues.

Question: Can the doctrine of collateral estoppel prevent a defendant from relitigating issues of fact decided against him by a judge in a prior proceeding even though he has a Seventh Amendment right to a jury trial in the second proceeding, but not the first, and even though the plaintiff, who was not involved in the prior suit, is the party seeking to invoke the doctrine?

Decision: Yes. Opinion by Justice Stewart. Vote: 8–1, Rehnquist dissenting.

Reasons: The Seventh Amendment right to jury trial is not violated by conferring collateral estoppel effects on determinations of fact made in equitable proceedings, even though the application of collateral estoppel has expanded from the confines existing in 1791 when the amendment was adopted. This conclusion was foreshadowed in *Katchen* v. *Landry,* 382 U.S. 323 (1966), and *Beacon Theatres* v. *Westover,* 359 U.S. 500 (1959), and is buttressed by the cardinal principle that procedural developments in areas defining the scope of the jury's function may not be rendered stillborn by the Seventh Amendment.

The evolution of collateral estoppel jurisprudence has been guided by twin purposes: protecting litigants from the burden of relitigating issues with the same party or a closely related one, and promoting judicial economy by forestalling needless litigation. These considerations anchored the holding in *Blonder-Tongue Laboratories, Inc.* v. *University of Illinois Foundation,* 402 U.S. 313 (1971), that a patentee may not relitigate the validity of a patent after a federal court in a previous lawsuit has declared it invalid. The virtues of a defendant's use of collateral estoppel blessed in *Blonder-Tongue,* however, are not fully present when collateral estoppel is wielded offensively by a plaintiff as in this case. The threat of defensive collateral estoppel encourages plaintiffs to join all potential defendants in a single lawsuit, whereas offensive use may spawn belated litigation animated by the hope of profiting from a previous judgment against the defendant. In addition, offensive use of collateral estoppel may be unfair if the defendant had little monetary or other incentive to defend vigorously, lacked procedural opportunities that might readily cause a different result at the subsequent trial, or had obtained favorable judgments inconsistent with the judgment relied upon as the foundation for the estoppel. Nevertheless,

> the preferable approach for dealing with these problems in the federal courts is not to preclude the use of offensive collateral estoppel, but to grant trial judges broad discretion to determine when it should be applied. The general rule should be that in cases where a plaintiff could easily have joined in the earlier action or where . . . the application of offensive collateral estoppel would be unfair to a defendant, a trial judge should not allow [its] use. . . .

In this case, circumstances are lacking that might preclude offensive use of collateral estoppel. The private plaintiffs had no right to join in the commission's lawsuit. The defendants had every incentive and opportunity to contest the commission's allegations vigorously, and their defeat by the commission was not inconsistent with any prior judgment. Finally, the private action offers the defendants no procedural opportunities not available in the commission's suit.

Montana v. *United States,* 440 U.S. 147 (1979)

Facts: At the behest and under the supervision of the United States, a contractor on a federal dam project in Montana brought suit in state court contending that the one percent gross receipts tax Montana exacted from contractors of public, but not private, construction projects was unconstitutional. The tax burden imposed solely on public contractors, it was urged, discriminated against the United States and the companies with which it dealt in violation of the supremacy clause, Article VI, clause 2 of the Constitution. The Montana Supreme Court sustained the gross receipts tax in *Peter Kiewit Sons' Co.* v. *State Board of Equalization (Kiewit I).* The contractor at first sought to appeal this decision to the U.S. Supreme Court but subsequently abandoned the request for review at the direction of the U.S. solicitor general. Instead, the contractor filed a second action in state court seeking a refund for certain tax payments different from those at issue in *Kiewit I.* After concluding that the second legal claim was in all material respects identical to the first, the Montana Supreme Court invoked the doctrines of collateral estoppel and former adjudication to affirm the dismissal of the complaint in *Peter Kiewit Sons' Co.* v. *Department of Revenue (Kiewit II).*

Less than a month after the contractor's initial complaint was filed in state court, the United States initiated a supremacy clause challenge to the constitutionality of Montana's gross receipts tax in federal district court. On stipulation by the parties, the federal court deferred decision until after the state litigation had been settled. Following the ruling in *Kiewit II*, however, the district court held that the tax unconstitutionally discriminated against the federal government or those with whom it transacts business. The contrary state court decision in *Kiewit I*, the district court asserted, did not foreclose its independent examination of the supremacy clause issue.

Question: Did the federal common law doctrine of collateral estoppel bar the United States from seeking a redetermination in federal district court of the adverse supremacy clause rulings issued in *Kiewit I* and *Kiewit II*?

Decision: Yes. Opinion by Justice Marshall. Vote: 8–1, White dissenting.

Reasons: Once an issue is actually and necessarily determined by a court of competent jurisdiction, the doctrine of collateral estoppel makes that determination conclusive in subsequent suits founded on a different cause of action involving the parties to the prior litigation. This collateral estoppel doctrine is also binding on nonparties who assume control over litigation in which they have a direct financial or proprietary interest and then seek to redetermine issues previously resolved. The United States exercised sufficient control over the *Kiewit I* lawsuit to activate principles of estoppel.

Resolution of the collateral estoppel defense raised in this case turns on three inquiries: whether the litigation presents issues identical in all materials respect to those resolved against the United States in *Kiewit I*; whether the state court judgment was postdated by significant changes in controlling facts or legal principles; and, whether other special circumstances warrant an exception to the normal rules of issue preclusion. The record and opinion in *Kiewit I* dispel any doubt that the Montana Supreme Court rejected the same supremacy clause attack that the United States unleashed in this case. It expressly addressed and disavowed the contention that the contested gross receipts tax on public contractors unconstitutionally discriminated against the federal government and federal contractors.

It is argued, however, that the factual predicate for *Kiewit I* was a contractual provision, absent here, that prohibited the federal contractor from offsetting the gross receipts tax with tax credits offered under Montana law. The record in this case demonstrates that after taking all credits available, federal contractors are still burdened by an effective gross revenue tax of one-half of 1 percent. A careful reading of the *Kiewit* opinions, moreover, reveals that the availability of tax credits to public contractors did not undergird the resolution of the supremacy clause question. Accordingly, no controlling facts have changed since *Kiewit I*. And no claim is made that new controlling legal principles have been proclaimed.

Finally, no special circumstances justify relieving the United States of the preclusive effects of estoppel. It voluntarily submitted the supremacy clause question to state courts and received a full and fair hearing there. In addition, the legal contentions raised in this case are so closely aligned in time and subject matter to those in *Kiewit I* that invocation of collateral estoppel will not ossify constitutional jurisprudence "where responsiveness to changing patterns of conduct or social mores is critical."

Douglas Oil Co. of California v. *Petrol Stops Northwest,* 441 U.S. 211 (1979)

Facts: Petrol Stops Northwest (Petrol Stops), an independent gasoline retailer, sued twelve large oil companies for alleged antitrust violations in an Arizona federal district court. A companion suit was filed by Gas-A-Tron of Arizona and Conoco against nine large oil companies. During pretrial discovery, the plaintiffs petitioned a California federal district court to release grand jury transcripts that might impeach an assertion of two defendants—Douglas Oil and Phillips Petroleum—that they had not communicated with competitors about the wholesale price of gasoline to independent retailers. The transcripts originated in a government investigation into price fixing of gasoline that resulted in an indictment and pleas of *nolo contendere* from these defendants. They had been disclosed to Douglas and Phillips before their pleas had been accepted by the district court.

Acting pursuant to rule 6(e) of the Federal Rules of Criminal Procedure, the California district court ordered disclosure subject to several protective conditions: transcript access was restricted to plaintiffs' counsel and for use in the civil litigation solely to impeach or refresh the recollection of witnesses; and plaintiffs were obliged to return the transcripts to the government after concluding all proper uses. The court of appeals affirmed the disclosure order.

Questions: (1) Did the California district court and court of appeals apply the correct legal standards in considering whether disclosure of the grand jury transcripts was proper under rule 6(e)? (2) Did the California district court, nevertheless, abuse its discretion in ordering disclosure without adequate knowledge of the status of and needs of the parties in the cognate Arizona civil suit where the transcripts were to be used?

Decision: Yes to both questions. Opinion by Justice Powell. Vote: 6–3, Stevens, Burger, and Stewart dissenting.

Reasons: Rule 6(e), as expounded in *United States* v. *Procter & Gamble*, 356 U.S. 677 (1958), and *Dennis* v. *United States*, 384 U.S. 855 (1961), permits disclosure of grand jury transcripts when an applicant demonstrates a need for the materials to avoid a possible injustice in another judicial proceeding, the need outweighs any interests advanced by continued secrecy, and the disclosure is limited to the needed materials. This standard applies whether or not the grand jury whose transcripts are sought has concluded its operations, although the termination diminishes the interests protected by continued secrecy. The district court and the court of appeals hewed to this standard in assessing the request for disclosure under rule 6(e).

The California district court, however, abused its broad discretion in ordering disclosure because it acted without sufficient information concerning the related civil suits pending in Arizona. To permit proper assessment of the continued need for grand jury secrecy, rule 6(e) requests should ordinarily be filed with the court that supervised the grand jury's activities. But where the requested material will be used in a different district court, the supervisory court may lack the information necessary to appraise the litigating needs of the applicant. In such situations, the supervisory court, after making a written evaluation of the need for continued grand jury secrecy and a determination that the limited evidence before it showed that disclosure might be appropriate, should send the requested materials to the court where the relevant litigation is pending for a final decision on the rule 6(e) request. This two-part procedure ensures that the offsetting needs for continued secrecy and disclosure are evaluated by the courts best equipped to do so. It need not be employed when the rule 6(e) issues can be accurately assessed without the review of the court presiding over the primary litigation. A two-part procedure was required in this case, however, because the California district court lacked dependable knowledge of the status of, and the needs of the parties in, the Arizona antitrust suits where the transcripts were to be used.

Helstoski v. Meanor, 442 U.S. 500 (1979)

Facts: A congressman was indicted on several counts for alleged corruption and bribery in introducing private bills on behalf of aliens that would permit them to remain in the country. He moved to dismiss the indictment on the ground that it violated the speech or debate clause of the Constitution, Article I, Section 6, clause 1. That clause, he argued, assigns exclusive jurisdiction over all legislative acts to Congress. The indictment offended the clause, he claimed, because it reflected an impermissible assertion of jurisdiction by the grand jury and the federal courts over the performance of his legislative prerogatives. The district court denied the motion, and the court of appeals rejected a petition for a writ of mandamus seeking dismissal of the indictment.

Question: Is mandamus an appropriate means of challenging the validity of an indictment of a congressman on the ground that it violates the speech or debate clause?

Decision: No. Opinion by Chief Justice Burger. Vote: 7–1, Brennan dissenting. Powell did not participate.

Reasons: A writ of mandamus may be issued only when there are no other channels for obtaining the requested relief. The speech or debate clause enshrines fundamental principles that reinforce the separation of powers among the three branches of government. It was designed to shield congressmen from the burden of defending themselves in courts for legislative acts. A final rejection of a speech or debate clause defense is collateral to the question of guilt or innocence and if not appealable under 28 U.S. Code 1291 would dilute the guarantees of the clause. We hold that if the congressman wished to challenge the denial of his motion to dismiss the indictment, direct appeal to the court of appeals rather than petitioning for a writ of mandamus was the proper course.

Labor Law

The Court displayed conflicting attitudes toward union power in twin decisions expounding the National Labor Relations Act. Augmenting the bargaining leverage of employees, a 6–3 majority upheld a state statute bestowing unemployment compensation on striking workers in *New York Telephone Co.* v. *New York State Department of Labor,* 440

U.S. 519 (1979). The norm of labor-management neutrality incorporated in the National Labor Relations Act, Justice Stevens declared, is not disturbed by an imbalance stemming from state programs of unemployment compensation. By a 5–4 margin in *NLRB* v. *Catholic Bishop of Chicago*, 440 U.S. 490 (1979), however, the Court ruled that the National Labor Relations Act's organizing and collective-bargaining protection does not extend to lay teachers employed by church-related schools.[1] Fearful of the excessive government entanglement with religion that a contrary conclusion might foster, the Court stated that the general language of the act was not intended to cover teachers closely allied with the inculcation of religious tenets.

New York Telephone Company v. *New York State Department of Labor*, 440 U.S. 519 (1979)

Facts: Under New York's general unemployment compensation law, striking workers are entitled to benefits after an eight-week waiting period. The benefits are funded in substantial part from employer contributions, and enhanced premiums are exacted from employers whose striking employees receive benefits. During a seven-month strike, employees of four Bell Telephone company affiliates in New York received more than $49 million in unemployment benefits. Thereafter, the companies obtained a declaratory judgment that federal labor law preempted the New York statute entitling striking workers to unemployment benefits and an award recouping the payments made because of the disbursement of funds to their striking employees. The availability of unemployment compensation to striking workers, the district court asserted, frustrates the federal policy of free collective bargaining by strengthening the economic leverage of labor. The court of appeals reversed, reasoning that Congress intended to tolerate the adoption of state unemployment compensation plans whether or not they contributed to the bargaining power of employees.

Question: Does federal labor law preempt New York's statute offering unemployment compensation to striking employees?

Decision: No. Plurality opinion by Justice Stevens. Vote: 6–3, Brennan, Blackmun, and Marshall concurring, Powell, Burger, and Stewart dissenting.

---

[1] Approximately 120,000 or 69 percent of the instructors employed by elementary and secondary Catholic schools are lay teachers.

Reasons: The legislative histories of the National Labor Relations Act and Title IX of the Social Security Act (which provides federal funds to states with qualifying unemployment compensation programs) evince a congressional intent to permit states broad freedom in designing unemployment compensation programs. In the absence of compelling congressional direction, therefore, it cannot be inferred that states have been barred from determining eligibility criteria for their unemployment compensation programs. Congress has failed to voice hostility toward the award of state unemployment benefits to striking employees, and "the fact that the implementation of this . . . policy affects the relative strength of the antagonists in a bargaining dispute is not a sufficient reason for concluding that Congress intended to pre-empt that exercise of State power."

NLRB v. *Catholic Bishop of Chicago,* 440 U.S. 490 (1979)

Facts: The National Labor Relations Board (NLRB) is charged with the responsibility of supervising union representation elections requested by employees of employers covered by section 2(2) of the National Labor Relations Act. Pursuant to this authority, the board ordered representation elections for lay teachers employed by Catholic schools that offered both religious and secular instruction. The employees voted in favor of representation by unions, but the schools refused either to recognize or to bargain with the unions. The board condemned this recalcitrance as an unfair labor practice, rejecting the contention that its jurisdiction over religious schools was either statutorily unauthorized or damaging to the religious freedom protected by the First Amendment. Denying enforcement of the unfair labor practice orders, the court of appeals concluded that the board's exercise of jurisdiction over church-related schools would violate the First Amendment by curtailing the freedom of church authorities to shape and direct teaching in accord with their religious tenets.

Question: Is the board empowered by the act to exercise jurisdiction over teachers employed by church-related schools to offer both religious and secular instructions?

Decision: No. Opinion by Chief Justice Burger. Vote: 5–4, Brennan, White, Marshall, and Blackmun dissenting.

Reasons: A fundamental precept of statutory construction goes against an interpretation that would give rise to serious constitutional questions. The exercise of jurisdiction by the board over lay teachers in church-related schools would threaten to give rise to excessive government entanglement with religion that could offend the First Amendment. Accordingly, the board should be denied such jurisdiction in the absence of a "clear expression of an affirmative intention of Congress that teachers in church-operated schools should be covered by the Act." An examination of both the terms of the act and its legislative history fails to disclose any such intent.

State Taxation and Regulation of Business

The 1978–1979 term witnessed nullification of state laws regulating the interstate sale of minnows and taxing foreign-owned cargo shipping containers used exclusively in international commerce. Overruling the octagenarian precedent of *Geer* v. *Connecticut,* 161 U.S. 519 (1896), the Court invalidated an Oklahoma statute making criminal the transport or shipment of minnows procured within the state to another state for sale (*Hughes* v. *Oklahoma,* 441 U.S. 332 [1979]). The commerce clause, Justice Brennan declared for a 7–2 majority, could not tolerate such blatant discrimination against interstate trade. Acknowledging a legitimate state interest in conserving minnows, Brennan explained that interstate commerce alone could not be saddled with restrictions defending this interest. The absence of any restrictions on the intrastate exploitation of minnows was fatal to the statute's constitutionality. The Court repudiated *Geer,* which had invested states with virtually complete power over wild animals within their jurisdictions on the theory that their citizens possessed common ownership of wildlife.

The commerce clause also frustrated California's quest to levy a personal property tax on cargo shipping containers owned by Japanese companies, employed exclusively on vessels registered and having their home ports in Japan, taxed in Japan, and devoted to international commerce. Speaking for an 8–1 majority in *Japan Line, Ltd.* v. *County of Los Angeles,* 441 U.S. 434 (1979), Justice Blackmun maintained that the tax flouted two commerce clause precepts: forestalling multiple taxation of the instrumentalities of foreign commerce; and federal uniformity in important matters affecting international trade.

Broad state power to experiment with economic regulation within their jurisdictions received constitutional endorsement in *New Motor Vehicle Board of California* v. *Orrin W. Fox Co.,* 439 U.S. 96 (1978). At issue was a state statute that mandated a delay in the establishment of new car dealerships within the marketing territory of an incumbent

155

franchisee if the latter voiced objection to the state motor vehicle board. Exonerating the automatic delay of an asserted procedural due process infirmity, the Court declared that rational economic regulation cannot be condemned simply because grievous losses are inflicted upon businessmen without a trial-type hearing. The Court further held that the anticompetitive effects of the disputed statute did not make it vulnerable to preemption under the Sherman Act.

Hughes v. *Oklahoma*, 441 U.S. 332 (1979)

Facts: An Oklahoma statute makes it a crime for any person to "transport or ship minnows for sale outside the state which were seized or procured within the waters of this state. . . ." A commercial minnow business operator was convicted under the statute for transporting to Texas natural minnows purchased in Oklahoma from a minnow dealer licensed to do business there. Oklahoma state courts rejected the operator's defense that the statute was constitutionally infirm under the commerce clause.

Question: Is the Oklahoma statute that curtails interstate commerce in natural minnows repugnant to the commerce clause?

Decision: Yes. Opinion by Justice Brennan. Vote: 7–2, Rehnquist and Burger dissenting.

Reasons: The commerce clause was inspired by a vision of national economic union, unfettered by protectionist policies of individual states. Even in the absence of congressional action, the clause preempts state laws that unduly burden interstate commerce.

The defendant contends that *Geer* v. *Connecticut*, 161 U.S. 519 (1896), constitutionally vindicates the contested Oklahoma statute. There the Court sustained a state statute that proscribed the interstate transportation of game birds that had been lawfully killed within the state. The Court had reasoned that a state, representing its citizens who "own" in common all wild animals, has power to control both the taking of game and any resulting claims of ownership. By virtue of common ownership, the Court continued, a state may keep within its jurisdiction the use of and commerce in wild animals. Cases postdating *Geer*, however, have disavowed its common ownership rationale in overturning state laws restricting the export of natural resources such as natural gas and shrimp. "We . . . conclude that challenges under the Commerce Clause to state regulations of wild animals should be considered according to the same general rule applied to state regulations of other natural resources, and therefore expressly overrule *Geer.*"

The general rule, as expounded in *Pike* v. *Bruce Church,* 397 U.S. 137 (1970), requires a threefold inquiry: whether the challenged statute discriminates against interstate commerce either on its face or in practical effect; whether it advances a legitimate local interest; and whether that interest could be safeguarded by alternative means without discriminating against interstate commerce. In this case, the questioned statute overtly discriminates against interstate commerce, since its proscription falls only on the transportation of natural minnows out of the state for purposes of sale. The statute furthers the legitimate local interest in the conservation and protection of wild animals, but it does so by exacting the full measure of conservation from interstate commerce. The number of natural minnows that can be taken by licensed dealers and their disposal within the state is unrestricted, although achievement of the state's conservation purpose would probably be more likely if restrictions on commerce in natural minnows applied evenhandedly to intrastate and interstate commerce. Accordingly, the statutory discrimination against the latter is unjustifiable under the commerce clause.

Japan Line, Ltd. v. *County of Los Angeles,* 441 U.S. 434 (1979)

Facts: Several counties and cities in California imposed a personal property tax on cargo shipping containers owned by Japanese shipping companies, incorporated under the laws of Japan and having their principal places of business there. The containers were used exclusively in foreign commerce, were employed on vessels registered and having their home ports in Japan, and were taxed in Japan. The California property taxes were founded on the temporary presence of the containers in California ports during loading, unloading, and repair work.

The Japanese companies paid the taxes under protest and sued for a refund in state court. The commerce clause of the U.S. Constitution, it was urged, preempted the exercise of local taxing power as applied to foreign-owned property devoted exclusively to international commerce. Noting the nondiscriminatory application of the property tax to both foreign and domestically owned containers, the California Supreme Court sustained its constitutionality.

Question: Does the commerce clause of the Constitution preempt application of California's property tax to the Japanese-owned cargo containers, employed solely in international commerce?

Decision: Yes. Opinion by Justice Blackmun. Vote: 8–1, Rehnquist dissenting.

Reasons: The commerce clause entrusts to Congress broad power over foreign commerce. In the absence of congressional action, moreover, it preempts state laws that threaten multiple taxation of foreign commerce or impairment of federal uniformity respecting important matters of international trade. These threats may be present even when the state tax is nondiscriminatory, fairly related to services provided by the taxing state, and founded on a substantial connection with the state.

When the subject of taxation is domiciled abroad, it may be fully taxed there. Any additional state tax, even if fairly apportioned, would expose the foreign company to multiple tax burdens that domestic commerce avoids. In addition, international tax disputes and foreign retaliation against American-owned instrumentalities may be triggered by applying state taxes to foreign-owned instrumentalities in international commerce. Such retaliation would not be restricted to the taxing state, and the whole nation would suffer. And if other states followed the taxing state's example, the problems of multiple taxation and balkanized regulation of foreign commerce would be compounded. In sum, the commerce clause cannot countenance state taxes on instrumentalities of foreign commerce that "create a substantial risk of international multiple taxation" or undermine federal uniformity in the regulation of commercial relations with foreign governments.

The disputed California property tax transgresses both of these commerce clause precepts. It exposes the Japanese-owned containers to multiple taxation because their full value is in fact subject to property tax in Japan. Uniform regulation of foreign trade is also jeopardized by the state tax. The United States and Japan are signatories to a customs convention on containers that encourages their use in international commerce by removing all duties and taxes on their temporary importation. Japan, moreover, eschews taxing American-owned containers. Imposition of the tax on Japanese-owned containers would, therefore, both risk retaliation by Japan and frustrate the federal policy of promoting the use of containers in foreign commerce. And if other states follow California's example, as Oregon has already done, these difficulties would be compounded.

California's property tax as applied to Japanese-owned containers is, therefore, twice-flawed under the commerce clause: it results in multiple taxation of the instrumentalities of foreign commerce; and it prevents the federal government from speaking with one voice in international trade.

New Motor Vehicle Board of California v. Orrin W. Fox Co., 439 U.S. 96 (1978)

Facts: A California statute limits the freedom of motor vehicle manufacturers to establish new dealerships within the market area of existing franchisees. If an incumbent franchisee files a timely protest with the motor vehicle board, the proposed competing dealership may not commence business until a hearing has been held and the board finds an absence of "good cause" for objecting to the dealership. A three-judge federal district court held that the statute's failure to offer the manufacturers and their proposed dealers a hearing prior to the mandated delay for commencing business offended the procedural due process required by the Fourteenth Amendment.

Question: Does due process condemn the statute's mandatory temporary delay at the behest of an incumbent auto dealer before the establishment of a competing dealership within his marketing territory?

Decision: No. Opinion by Justice Brennan. Vote 8–1, Stevens dissenting.

Reasons: No procedural due process concerns are raised by the statute's temporary delay of the establishment of auto dealerships pending the board's adjudication of the protests of incumbent dealers. Procedural due process protections safeguard a person's interest in the reliable determination of adjudicative facts that could adversely affect constitutionally protected liberty or property interests. But they offer no shield against rational legislative determinations to enact economic regulation of the type at issue in this case. The contested statute reflects a reasonable accommodation among the conflicting economic interests of automobile manufacturers, their prospective franchisees, and incumbent dealers. "Once having enacted a reasonable general scheme of business regulation, California was not required to provide for a prior individualized hearing each and every time the provisions of the [statute] had the effect of delaying consummation of the business plans of particular individuals." The political process is the only recourse available to mitigate the effects of rational regulatory statutes that may visit economic hardship on particular individuals.

It is argued that the statute impermissibly delegates state power to a private citizen because its mandatory delay provision may be triggered only at the behest of incumbent dealers who may decline to invoke their right of protest. But this feature is characteristic of almost any system of private law. "An otherwise valid regulation is not rendered invalid simply because those whom the regulation is designed to safeguard may waive its protection."

Finally, it is argued that the statute is preempted by the Sherman Act because it empowers private individuals to impose restraints on trade. The statute embodies a clearly articulated and affirmatively expressed legislative choice, however, to displace unfettered business freedom with respect to the establishment of new auto dealerships. The duration of any delay and the ultimate decision whether to approve a new dealership rests solely in the hands of the motor vehicle board. The statute is, therefore, exempt from Sherman Act scrutiny under the "state action" doctrine of *Parker* v. *Brown*, 317 U.S. 341 (1943). Although the statute may dampen intrabrand competition between auto dealers, anticompetitive effects alone do not condemn state laws under the Sherman Act. Otherwise, states would be virtually powerless to engage in economic regulation.

Federal Regulation: Antitrust, Patents, Securities, Environment, and Freedom of Information

The 1978–1979 term brought a spate of decisions expounding cardinal federal regulatory and disclosure statutes. In the field of antitrust, the Court refused to condemn blanket licenses of copyrighted musical compositions as offensive per se to the Sherman Act (*Broadcast Music, Inc.* v. *CBS, Inc.*, 441 U.S. 1 [1979]). Disavowing an unreflective concept of price fixing espoused by the Second Circuit, the Court unanimously agreed that the licenses should be examined under a "rule of reason." The "business of insurance," shielded from antitrust scrutiny by the McCarran-Ferguson Act, was narrowly interpreted in *Group Life & Health Ins. Co.* v. *Royal Drug Co., Inc.*, 440 U.S. 205 (1979). A 5–4 majority ruled that provider agreements with insurance companies are presumptively outside the antitrust exemption bestowed by the act. The Court also endorsed a narrow construction of the Robinson-Patman Act in *Great A&P Tea Co.* v. *FTC*, 440 U.S. 69 (1979). A buyer cannot be assailed as a knowing beneficiary of price discrimination, the Court held, if the seller could successfully interpose a defense to any legal action initiated against it.

An excursion into federal patent law came in *Aronson* v. *Quick Point Pencil Co.*, 440 U.S. 257 (1979). There a unanimous Court perceived no preemptive conflict between the threefold aims of patent policy and a contractual arrangement to pay royalties on the sale of an article ultimately denied a patent.

The Court twice stepped into the forest of federal securities laws to echo sentiments voiced in recent terms[1] against expansive growth by judicial husbandry. By an 8–0 vote the Court held that an employee's interest in a noncontributory, compulsory pension plan is outside the protections attached to a "security" in the Securities Acts. (*International Brotherhood of Teamsters* v. *Daniel*, 439 U.S. 551 [1979]). And courts were admonished in *Touche Ross & Co.* v. *Redington*, 442 U.S. 560 (1979) against unthinking implication of private rights of action to protect policies enshrined in the Securities Acts. Specifically, a 7–1 majority declared, section 17(a) of the Securities Exchange Act does not endow private parties with the right to question accountants for certifying allegedly misleading financial statements filed by brokers with the Securities and Exchange Commission.

Application of the omnipresent National Environmental Policy Act to the federal appropriations process was contested in *Andrus* v. *Sierra Club*, 442 U.S. 347 (1979). A unanimous Court held that federal agencies may submit appropriations requests without preparing environmental impact statements.

The Freedom of Information Act requires public disclosure of federal agency records, subject to nine specified exemptions. The Court held in *Chrysler Corp.* v. *Brown*, 441 U.S. 281 (1979), that the exemptions are permissive rather than mandatory restraints on disclosure. However, the Court held, the Administrative Procedure Act might prohibit disclosure of agency records that violate other statutes, such as the Trade Secrets Act.

The buying and selling of government securities to implement national monetary policy precipitated a Freedom of Information dis-

---

[1] See Piper Aircraft Corp. v. Chris-Craft Industries, Inc., 430 U.S. 1 (1977) (no private damage action for tender offerers injured either by misleading statements made in violation of the Williams Act or by manipulation of the market in violation of rule 10b-6 issued pursuant to the Securities Exchange Act); Blue Chip Stamps v. Manor Drug Stores, Inc., 427 U.S. 723 (1975) (no private right of action under rule 10b-5 promulgated pursuant to the Securities Exchange Act for nonpurchasers or nonsellers); United Housing Foundation v. Forman, 421 U.S. 837 (1975) (stock in a housing cooperative is not a security protected by the Securities Acts); Santa Fe Industries, Inc. v. Green, 430 U.S. 462 (1977) (rule 10b-5 powerless to rectify breaches of fiduciary duties that majority shareholders owe to the minority).

pute in *Federal Open Market Committee* v. *Merrill,* 443 U.S. 340 (1979). Prompt disclosure was sought of monthly directives issued by the Federal Reserve System to guide its participation in the market for government securities. Objection was lodged because immediate disclosure would assertedly confound incremental changes in monetary policy and disadvantage small investors. A 7–2 Court majority ruled that belated disclosure of the directives could be justified under exemption 5 of the act (protecting intra-agency memorandums not available by law to a party in litigation with the agency), if necessary to forestall significant harm to the government's monetary functions or to commercial interests.

Broadcast Music, Inc. v. *CBS, Inc.,* 441 U.S. 1 (1979)

Facts: Columbia Broadcasting System, Inc. (CBS) brought suit against the American Society of Composers, Authors and Publishers (ASCAP) and Broadcast Music, Inc. (BMI), assailing the legality of blanket licenses to copyrighted musical compositions at fees negotiated by the organizations. ASCAP was conceived to assist composers of copyrighted music in preventing unauthorized use of their compositions under the copyright laws. At present, 22,000 composers are members of ASCAP, all of whom grant it nonexclusive rights to license nondramatic performances of their work. ASCAP issues licenses and distributes royalties to copyright owners. BMI, a nonprofit corporation, is affiliated with or represents some 10,000 publishing companies and 20,000 authors and composers. Its operations resemble those of ASCAP. Virtually every domestic copyrighted composition is in the repertory either of ASCAP, with 3 million compositions, or of BMI, with 1 million.

Both organizations predominately employ blanket licenses, which authorize licensees to perform any and all compositions owned by the members or affiliates without limit for a specified duration. Fees for blanket licenses are ordinarily a percentage of total revenues or a flat dollar amount and are unaffected by the amount or type of music used. CBS alleged, among other things, that the blanket license constituted price fixing and offended the Sherman Act's proscription against unreasonable trade restraints. After a lengthy trial, the district court dismissed the complaint. Since prospective television network licensees could negotiate directly with individual copyright owners if a blanket license was unwanted, the court declared, any trade restraints exacted by a blanket license were reasonable. The court of appeals reversed, holding that the blanket license issued to television networks was a form of price fixing illegal per se under the Sherman Act.

Question: Did the court of appeals err in holding that the blanket license was per se illegal under the Sherman Act?

Decision: Yes. Opinion by Justice White. Vote: 9–0.

Reasons: The Sherman Act condemns only unreasonable restraints of trade. Certain agreements or practices are so plainly anticompetitive and so often lacking in offsetting competitive virtues that they are conclusively presumed illegal under the Sherman Act without further examination. This per se rule adds desirable clarity to Sherman Act prohibitions and obviates protracted and complex inquiries into the economics of numerous industries.

Agreements among competitors to fix the prices of their individual goods or services are proscribed under the per se rule. CBS contends that the blanket licenses of ASCAP and BMI are likewise tainted because they result from a combination of composers and publishing houses into an organization that sets a price for performing competing copyrighted compositions. But a per se prohibition of the blanket license can be justified only if considerable experience has revealed anticompetitive effects that are unequivocal and clearly have no legitimate business purpose.

The views of the Department of Justice and provisions in the Copyright Act of 1976 indicate that blanket licenses in some circumstances may be economically beneficial. The vast numbers using copyrighted music, the ease with which a performance may be broadcast, the volume of copyrighted compositions, the number and ephemeral nature of separate performances, and the impracticability of negotiating individual licenses for each composition—all create unique market conditions for performance rights to recorded music. Performing rights to copyrighted music, moreover, exist solely because of the copyright laws. A user of copyrighted music in a public performance must secure consent from the copyright owner or pay statutory damages for each infringement. Market arrangements reasonably necessary to protect rights conferred by the copyright laws should not unreflectively be brought within the per se rule.

In addition, the practical considerations that spurred the use of the blanket licenses confirm their legitimate business function. The blanket license arose from the desire of users for unplanned, rapid and indemnified access to any and all of a broad repertory of compositions, and the desire of owners for a reliable method of collecting for the use of their copyrighted works. Individual copyright negotiations would be expensive, as would monitoring and enforcement by single composers. ASCAP and BMI were created to perform the role of middlemen and utilize a blanket license to forestall the prohibitive costs of individual negotiations and enforcement. This substantial lowering of costs is potentially beneficial to both buyers and sellers.

The blanket license also has unique characteristics: it offers the licensee immediate use of covered compositions, flexibility in the choice of musical material, and escape from the inevitable delays and costs associated with individual negotiations. To the extent that a blanket license has special attributes, ASCAP and BMI cannot be equated with joint selling agencies offering the individual goods of competitors; rather, the license is a unique product of which individual compositions are raw material but which cannot be duplicated by individual composers.

Finally, the blanket license does not prevent all price competition for copyrighted music. The district court found that neither legal, practical, nor conspiratorial obstacles would confront CBS if it chose to negotiate individual licenses with members of ASCAP or BMI.

In sum, there is no foundation for concluding that blanket licenses inexorably threaten competition without redeeming market virtues. Therefore, they should not be rejected as illegal per se, but should be examined under the rule of reason to determine whether they can survive Sherman Act scrutiny.

Group Life & Health Insurance Co. v. Royal Drug Co., Inc., 440 U.S. 205 (1979)

Facts: With limited exceptions, section 2(b) of the McCarran-Ferguson Act, 15 U.S. Code 1012(b), shields the "business of insurance" from the scrutiny of antitrust laws. A federal district court held that section 2(b) conferred antitrust immunity on provider agreements between Blue Shield of Texas and certain participating pharmacies. The agreements obligate the latter to furnish prescription drugs to Blue Shield policyholders at $2.00 for each prescription in return for Blue Shield's payment of the costs of acquiring the amount of the drug prescribed. The court of appeals reversed, concluding that the pharmacy agreements were not the "business of insurance" within the meaning of section 2(b).

Question: Did the court of appeals err in holding that the pharmacy provider agreements were not the "business of insurance"?

Decision: No. Opinion by Justice Stewart. Vote: 5–4, Brennan, Marshall, Burger, and Powell dissenting.

Reasons: The starting point for resolving a question of statutory construction is the language of the statute itself. It is notable, therefore, that section 2(b) exempts the "business of insurance" but not the business of insurance companies.

The core elements of an insurance contract are "the spreading and underwriting of a policyholder's risks." In contrast, the pharmacy agreements at issue reflect mere arrangements by Blue Shield to purchase goods and services. Although such arrangements may reduce Blue Shield's costs and redound to the benefit of policyholders in the form of lower premiums, they are not the "business of insurance." This conclusion is reinforced by the common understanding that the business of insurance is marked by the contract between the insurer and the insured. Moreover, the legislative history of the McCarran-Ferguson Act and the well-settled rule that exemptions from the antitrust laws are to be narrowly construed counsel against an expansive conception of section 2(b). In sum, there is no persuasive evidence that Congress intended the "business of insurance" to embrace contracts between insurance companies and providers of goods and services, even if they reduce the costs of satisfying underwriting obligations to policyholders.

Great A & P Tea Co. v. FTC, 440 U.S. 69 (1979)

Facts: Seeking to maintain its large milk supply account with the Great Atlantic and Pacific Tea Company (A&P), the Borden Company offered to reduce its price by $410,000 annually. A competitor of Borden, however, submitted an offer to A&P that was some $300,000 below Borden's price. Thereafter, A&P informed Borden of the competing bid, but declined to disclose specifically by what amount it undercut Borden's price, indicating only that the amount was far in excess of $50,000. Borden then submitted a new bid, accepted by A&P, which doubled the initial discount offer from $410,000 to $820,000 a year and beat the competitor's bid by almost $100,000. This transaction inspired the Federal Trade Commission to charge A&P with a violation of section 2(f) of the Robinson-Patman Act, which

165

proscribes the knowing inducement or receipt of illegal price discrimination. After an extensive hearing, the commission found that Borden had discriminated in price between A&P and its competitors, that the discrimination had been injurious to competition, and that A&P knew or should have known that it was the beneficiary of unlawful price discrimination. Accordingly, the commission sustained the section 2(f) charge, rejecting A&P's argument that its prohibitory ambit did not reach price discriminations by sellers whose conduct was beyond Robinson-Patman Act reproach. The court of appeals affirmed.

Question: Did section 2(f) of the act condemn A&P for inducing or receiving a price discrimination from Borden that the latter was legally entitled to offer under the Robinson-Patman Act?

Decision: No. Opinion by Justice Stewart. Vote: 6–2, White and Marshall dissenting in part.

Reasons: Section 2(f) imposes liability on buyers for knowingly inducing or receiving a discrimination in price "which is prohibited by this section." Although the phrase "this section" refers to the entire section 2 of the act, it derives significance from subsections (a) and (b) dealing with price discriminations by sellers. The plain meaning of section 2(f), fortified by legislative history, compels the conclusion that buyer liability is dependent on seller liability under section 2(a). Accordingly, A&P was shielded from liability if Borden's discrimination in price was legally protected by an affirmative defense under section 2(b).

That section exonerates a seller from liability if its discrimination in price stemmed from a good faith belief that a price concession was necessary to meet an equally low price of a competitor.

> Since good faith, rather than absolute certainty, is the touchstone of the meeting competition defense, a seller can assert the defense even if it has unknowingly made a bid that in fact not only met but beat his competition.

In this case, Borden's $820,000 price concession to A&P was clearly triggered by a reasonable belief that it was necessary to maintain A&P's patronage and to meet a competitor's bid. Borden made reasonable, albeit unsuccessful, efforts to ascertain the precise details of the competing bid. The conclusion is virtually inescapable that Borden's discount price to A&P reflected a good faith effort to meet competition and was thus insulated from liability by the meeting-competition defense. Borden's defense offered a corresponding shield to A&P against buyer liability under section 2(f).

Whether a buyer who induces price concessions from a seller through deliberate misrepresentations may escape section 2(f) liability, even if the seller has a meeting-competition defense, is a question that need not be confronted in this case.

Aronson v. Quick Point Pencil Co., 440 U.S. 257 (1979)

Facts: Aronson sought a patent for a new form of keyholder. During the pendency of the application, she negotiated a contract with the Quick Point Pencil Company for the manufacture and sale of the keyholder. It required Quick Point initially to pay a 5 percent royalty on gross sales, reduced to 2½ percent if a patent was not granted within five years. After the application was denied, Quick Point paid the 2½ percent royalty for fourteen years. Thereafter, it brought suit claiming that federal patent law rendered the royalty agreement unenforceable. The district court rejected the claim, but the court of appeals reversed. The strong federal policy favoring open exploitation of ideas in the public domain, the court declared, required invalidation of the royalty contract once the patent application was denied. The court noted, moreover, the royalty obligation would have expired after seventeen years if a patent was granted and would have been nullified if the patent was subsequently declared invalid.

Question: Does federal patent law preclude enforcement of contractual obligations to pay royalties to a patent applicant on sales of articles incorporating the putative invention if a patent is not granted?

Decision: No. Opinion by Chief Justice Burger. Vote: 9–0.

Reasons: The preemptive ambit of federal patent law reaches only those state contractual obligations whose enforcement would undermine congressional objectives. The purposes of the federal patent system are threefold: to foster and reward invention; to promote disclosure of inventions so that further innovation may ensue and public exploitation may be permitted once the patent expires; and to ensure that unpatentable ideas in the public domain remain there for free use. Enforcement of the 2½ percent royalty agreement does not upset these aims.

Permitting such agreements offers an incentive to innovation. The royalty contract at issue, moreover, encouraged Aronson to arrange for the manufacture of her keyholder and thereby advanced

167

the federal policy of disclosure; the devices display the novel idea they embody wherever they are seen. Enforcing the royalty agreement will not withdraw any idea from the public domain since the design of the keyholder remained confidential until Quick Point obtained its manufacturing license. Finally, inventors will not be deterred from seeking patents in the hope of maximizing profits if the 2½ percent royalty obligation is enforced. If Aronson was awarded a patent, her 5 percent royalty would have expired after the seventeen-year life of the patent, possibly supplemented by payments from licenses other than Quick Point's. Whether that patent exploitation would have been less profitable to Aronson than the indefinite 2½ percent royalty agreement with Quick Point is speculative.

International Brotherhood of Teamsters v. Daniel, 439 U.S. 551 (1979)

Facts: A multi-employer collective bargaining agreement between a local teamsters union and trucking firms established a compulsory and noncontributory pension plan for employees represented by the union. Employer contributions to the pension fund were tied to the number of employees. Twenty years of continuous service was required to qualify for a pension. Denied benefits under the pension plan because of a single, short-lived involuntary break in employment over a twenty-three year period, an employee brought suit against the union alleging, among other things, violations of section 10(b) of the Securities Exchange Act of 1934 and section 17(a) of the Securities Act of 1933 (Securities Acts). The complaint alleged that the employee's interest in the pension fund constituted a "security" within the ambit of the Securities Acts and that the failure of the union to disclose material facts relevant to the value of that security constituted a fraud in connection with its sale to the employee. The union moved to dismiss the securities claims, contending that the pension fund interest was not a security governed by the Securities Acts. The district court denied the motion, and the court of appeals affirmed.

Question: Is an employee's interest in a noncontributory, compulsory pension plan a "security" within the meaning of the Securities Acts?

Decision: No. Opinion by Justice Powell. Vote: 8–0, Stevens did not participate.

Reasons: Rules of statutory construction and prior decisions expounding the meaning of the term "security" in the Securities Acts refute the argument that noncontributory, compulsory pension plans are securities within their purview. Both statutes conspicuously omit reference to pension plans in defining the term "security." It is said, however, that an employee's interest in a pension plan is an "investment contract," an instrument embraced by the statutory definition of a security.

In *United Housing Corp.* v. *Forman,* 421 U.S. 823 (1975), and *SEC* v. *W. J. Howey Co.,* 328 U.S. 293 (1946), the Court confined the term investment contract to those financial relationships involving an investment of money in a common enterprise premised on a reasonable expectation of profits derived from the entrepreneurial or managerial efforts of others. An employee's interest in a compulsory, noncontributory pension fund is twice-flawed as an investment contract. First, the employee does not invest his money in the fund; he accepts employment for wages coupled with a possibility of receiving a pension upon retirement. In any realistic sense, the employee "is selling labor to obtain a livelihood, not making an investment in the future." Second, any investment the employee made in the pension fund was not founded on an expectation of profit derived from the management of the fund. Employer contributions to the fund dwarfed the significance of earnings derived from investing its assets. In addition, the principal barrier to obtaining benefits from the fund is not its financial health or investment profits, but satisfying exacting eligibility requirements.

When viewed in light of the total compensation package an employee must receive in order to be eligible for pension benefits, it becomes clear that the possibility of participating in a plan's asset earnings "is far too speculative and insubstantial to bring the entire transaction within the Securities Acts."

The passage of the Employee Retirement Income Security Act of 1974 confirms the view that noncontributory compulsory pension plans are outside the Securities Acts. It regulates expressly and in detail employee pension plans, including plan obligations with respect to disclosure and eligibility requirements. This comprehensive legislation bespeaks a congressional understanding that ERISA was necessary to fill a regulatory void.

Touche Ross & Co. v. *Redington,* 442 U.S. 560 (1979)

Facts: Section 17(a) of the Securities Exchange Act of 1934 requires brokerage firms that transact business through a national securities exchange to maintain such records and to make such reports as the Securities and Exchange Commission prescribes as appropriate in the public interest or for the protection of investors. By regulation, the commission obligates brokerage firms within the ambit of section 17(a) to file annual reports, certified by an independent public accountant, that disclose their financial condition. Following the insolvency and liquidation of Weis Securities, Inc., a member of the New York Stock Exchange, suit was brought under section 17(a) against Touche Ross & Co., the certified public accountant that had audited Weis's books and prepared its annual financial reports for filing with the commission. Touche Ross, the complaint alleged, improperly audited and certified Weis's 1972 misleading financial statements that concealed substantial operating losses. The district court dismissed the complaint, stating that no private cause of action could be implied from section 17(a). The court of appeals, however, reversed.

Question: Does section 17(a) create a private cause of action to rectify misstatements contained in obligatory financial reports filed with the commission?

Decision: No. Opinion by Justice Rehnquist. Vote: 7–1, Marshall dissenting, Powell not participating.

Reasons: The basis for determining the existence of a federal statutory cause of action is the intent of Congress. The language of the statute itself begins the analysis. Nothing in section 17(a) either confers rights on private parties or proscribes particular conduct. It simply requires the maintenance and filing of certain records and reports to assist the commission in policing the securities industry. The information disclosed in section 17(a) reports is intended to disclose incipient signs of financial deterioration to the commission that could threaten investors unless remedial action is undertaken. In sum, the architects of section 17(a) sought to forestall bankruptcy, not to compensate its victims by offering a private damage action.

The legislative history of section 17(a) is mute on the question of whether a private damage action should be implied to redress the wrongdoing alleged in this case. This silence reinforces the negative conclusion mandated by an ordinary reading of the statutory terms. It speaks volumes, moreover, that Congress embraced explicit language to create private rights of action in other sections of the Securities Exchange Act.

The language, purpose, and legislative history of section 17(a), therefore, unmistakably counsel against implying a private cause of action. Where congressional intent from these sources is so apparent, further inquiry into whether an implied private remedy is necessary to the purpose of the statute or whether the alleged cause of action is one traditionally relegated to state law would be pointless.

It is asserted, nonetheless, that to deny private damage actions under section 17(a) sanctions injustice. Even assuming the accuracy of the assertion, the Constitution has not crowned this Court with authority to repair what it perceives are statutory flaws.

Andrus v. *Sierra Club*, 442 U.S. 347 (1979)

Facts: Section 102(c) of the National Environmental Policy Act obligates all federal agencies to prepare environmental impact statements (EIS) in connection with proposals for legislation and regarding major federal actions "significantly affecting the quality of the human environment." In a decision expounding the application of section 102(c) to the appropriations process, a federal appeals court held that an EIS must be prepared whenever a federal agency requests an appropriation from Congress either in conjunction with a proposal for new action or to underwrite a programmatic course.

Question: Does the NEPA require the preparation of EISs to accompany appropriation requests from federal agencies?

Decision: No. Unanimous opinion by Justice Brennan.

Reasons: The EIS obligation of section 102(c) applies only to "proposals for legislation" or "proposals for major Federal actions." An appropriation request is not proposed "legislation" for purposes of section 102(c). The Council on Environmental Quality, charged with overseeing the NEPA, has embraced this view, which is confirmed by the deeply ingrained congressional distinction between "legislation" and "appropriation."

Appropriation requests are excluded from the ambit of proposals for major federal actions because they do not "propose"; rather, they fund action already proposed. To conclude otherwise would beget a proliferation of EISs that simply parrot those prepared for the underlying programs to be funded. Canons of statutory construction counsel against such redundancy.

Chrysler Corp. v. *Brown*, 441 U.S. 281 (1979)

Facts: The Chrysler Corporation, a contractor with the federal government, filed an affirmative action program and related information reports with the Defense Logistic Agency (DLA). The filings were required by regulations promulgated by the Department of Labor to implement Executive Order 11246. One regulation provides that public disclosure of affirmative action programs and reports will be made, even though not required under the Freedom of Information Act (FOIA), if it furthers the public interest without frustrating federal enforcement functions. But the regulation does provide an exception to this policy where disclosure is prohibited by law.

Third parties made FOIA requests seeking from the DLA certain affirmative action records filed by Chrysler. Informed of prospective release of the reports, Chrysler sought an injunction against disclosure in federal district court. Disclosure was prohibited, Chrysler asserted, under the FOIA, certain federal confidentiality statutes, and the Administrative Procedure Act. After a trial *de novo*, the district court granted the injunction. Finding that some of the requested information fell within exemption 4 of the FOIA, the district court concluded, nevertheless, that an exemption from the information act's disclosure obligation did not rule out voluntary agency disclosure. The district court declared, however, that the requested records were protected from disclosure under the APA by virtue of 18 U.S. Code 1905. That section imposes criminal sanctions on government employees who make unauthorized disclosure of trade secrets or confidential statistical data.

The court of appeals vacated and remanded. It agreed that neither an exemption to the FOIA nor confidentiality statutes prohibited agency disclosure of the records at issue. It disagreed, however, with the district court's application of the APA.

Questions: (1) Do FOIA exemptions forbid agencies from voluntarily disclosing information within their protective ambits? (2) Does 18 U.S. Code 1905 create a private right of action to enjoin violations of its criminal sanctions? (3) Would agency disclosure of information protected by section 1905 constitute an abuse of discretion proscribed by the APA?

Decision: No to questions 1 and 2 and yes to question 3. Opinion by Justice Rehnquist for a unanimous Court.

Reasons: The FOIA requires public disclosure of any agency record, subject to nine specified exemptions. Its structure and legislative history unequivocally demonstrate that its exemptions were not intended to curtail an agency's discretion to disclose information. Thus,

Chrysler lacked any right under the FOIA to enjoin disclosure of the affirmative action records at issue.

The Trade Secrets Act, 18 U.S. Code 1905, however, makes it a crime for a government employee to disclose trade secrets or confidential statistical data "to any extent not authorized by law." The court of appeals concluded that the Labor Department regulation permitting disclosure of affirmative action information constituted "law" within the meaning of section 1905. That conclusion is untenable.

The language and history of section 1905 demonstrate that it limits formal agency action and is not simply a proscription against leaks. And agency regulations do not acquire the force and effect of law unless they have certain substantive characteristics and were antedated by certain procedural formalities. Regulations must implement a statutory mandate to attain the force of law. The thread between the Labor Department regulations relied on by the court of appeals and "any grant of authority by the Congress is so strained that it would do violence to established principles of separation of powers to denominate these particular regulations 'legislative' and credit them with the 'binding effect of law.' " Moreover, the regulations were not issued in conformity with the procedural requirements for substantive rule making under the APA. The regulations, thus, are not "law" within the intendment of section 1905. There is no foundation, however, for implying a private right of action in favor of Chrysler to challenge unlawful disclosure under that section.

On the other hand, Chrysler can invoke the judicial review protections against wayward agency action afforded by the APA. That statute permits any person "adversely affected or aggrieved" by agency action to obtain judicial review. The reviewing court is instructed to set aside any action "not in accordance with law." If the records at issue were barred from disclosure under section 1905, their release would violate the APA. The court of appeals should address the applicability of section 1905 to the contested records on remand.

Federal Open Market Committee v. Merrill, 443 U.S. 340 (1979)

Facts: The Federal Open Market Committee of the Federal Reserve System meets monthly to review the nation's monetary policy. Its principal conclusions are incorporated in a Domestic Policy Directive, which discloses whether short-term interest rates or money supply targets should be changed. The monthly directive guides the Federal Reserve System in the purchase and sale of government securities to carry out monetary policy. A directive is withheld from the public for one month, when its authority is eclipsed by a superseding directive.

Suit was filed seeking prompt disclosure of each directive under the Freedom of Information Act, 5 U.S. Code 552. The committee voiced two objections against immediate disclosure: that it would impede incremental changes in monetary policy as market participants rushed to adjust their security holdings in anticipation of purchases or sales by the Federal Reserve System; and that large, sophisticated institutional investors would obtain an unfair market advantage over small investors. The district court ordered immediate disclosure of the directives, explaining that they were statements of general agency policy under 5 U.S. Code 552(a)(1)(D) that must be currently published in the Federal Register for the guidance of the public. Affirming, the court of appeals rejected the committee's contention that exemption 5 of the act, 5 U.S. Code 552(b)(5), shielded the directives from immediate disclosure.

Question: Does exemption 5 of the act permit belated disclosure of the committee's directives if necessary to forestall significant harm to the government's monetary functions or commercial interests?

Decision: Yes. Opinion by Justice Blackmun. Vote: 7–2, Stevens and Stewart dissenting.

Reasons: Generally speaking, the act entitles any person to disclosure of federal agency records, subject to nine specified exemptions. Exemption 5 permits withholding of "inter-agency or intra-agency memorandums or letters which would not be available by law to a party . . . in litigation with the agency." The directives at issue are clearly intra-agency memorandums of the committee. Whether they would be available by law to a party in litigation with the committee is problematic.

Past decisions expounding exemption 5 have established that memoranda constituting either a privileged attorney's work product or predecisional deliberations protected by executive privilege fall within its ambit. The committee contends that commercial information whose public disclosure can be limited under rule 26(c)(7) of the Federal Rules of Civil Procedures should also be protected by exemption 5. We agree.

That rule empowers federal district courts for "good cause shown" to restrict the disclosure of confidential "commercial information." The legislative history of exemption 5 discloses modest support for a qualified privilege for confidential commercial information of the type generated by the government in contract negotiations. The committee's directives are analogous to such information since they relate to the buying and selling of securities in the open market. Accordingly, if belated disclosure of the directives would be proper under rule 26(c)(7), exemption 5 would authorize the practice.

There is only a qualified privilege against the immediate disclosure of confidential commercial information during civil discovery. The privilege may be invoked only when disclosure would inflict harms that outweigh the need for immediate release. Applying this balance, the committee's directive would be protectable against immediate disclosure only if it "would significantly harm the Government's monetary functions or commercial interests." The case must be remanded to determine whether the committee can establish the requisite harm needed to afford the directives qualified protection in civil discovery.

INDEX OF CASES
1978–1979 Term

(See page 183 for an index of cases in the previous seven volumes of Significant Decisions of the Supreme Court, covering the years 1971 to 1978.)

SUBJECT INDEX
1978–1979 Term

INDEX OF CASES
1971–1978

This index covers all cases that have been summarized in the previous seven volumes of Significant Decisions of the Supreme Court. *(For the 1978–1979 term, see the index of cases on page 176.) The term in which each case was argued indicates the volume in which it is discussed; indexes within each volume give page references for the discussion.*

195